Practical Percussion

A Guide to the Instruments and Their Sources

James Holland

The Scarecrow Press, Inc.
Lanham, Maryland, and Oxford
2003

SCARECROW PRESS, INC.

Published in the United States of America
by Scarecrow Press, Inc.
A Member of the Rowman & Littlefield Publishing Group
4501 Forbes Boulevard, Suite 200, Lanham, Maryland 20706
www.scarecrowpress.com

P.O. Box 317
Oxford
OX2 9RU, UK

British Library Cataloguing in Publication Information Available

Library of Congress Cataloging-in-Publication Data

Holland, James, 1933–
  Practical percussion : a guide to the instruments and their sources /
James Holland.
      p.   cm.
Includes bibliographical references (p.) and index.
  ISBN 0-8108-4395-1 (alk. paper)
1. Percussion instruments. I. Title.
ML1030 .H65 2002
786.8—dc21   2002026843

CONTENTS

FOREWORD

In the orchestral repertoire and even more in chamber music, the percussion section was for long the poor relation, used mainly for purposes of illustration or anecdote as if merely to underline an important moment: triangle, bass drum, tabor, and cymbals were the main resources. Only timpani had attained the rank of instrumental nobility, their use sanctified by baroque and classical music. The great Romantic composers used percussion sparingly to the extent that developments had to wait until the beginning of the twentieth century. Stravinsky's *Histoire du Soldat* marked a major development, influenced as the composer was by early jazz recordings. These, more than any so-called classical music, contributed to the emancipation of percussion and to its rise to its current prominent position in the orchestral landscape.

Those classical instruments, still in daily use today, hardly changed for decades, even centuries. They found their definitive form and function early on. Even if their usage evolved and developed according to new techniques of composition, their production and diffusion of sound have now been definitively established. The same cannot be said of percussion instruments that proliferate endlessly in a sort of anarchy. Why is this? Whereas our classical instruments derive from the western tradition, even though they may have originated in other more distant civilizations and cultures, percussion instruments derive mainly from diverse traditions with very different acoustic requirements to our own. We have imported them without concerning ourselves overmuch with the contexts from which they emerge. Thus we all have a lot to learn about and with them.

The first necessity is of course to establish a catalogue of instruments according to families, materials, and methods of playing. For pitched instruments, even relatively complex ones, the task is made easier by virtue of the fact that one can refer to precise scales. For unpitched instruments, we have recourse to only much vaguer categories. Furthermore, if one has never heard a rare percussion instrument, how is one to imagine it without an example of its sound?

The richness and diversity of percussion instruments have still to be fully explored, but we can now begin to appreciate the recent growth in their role and importance in the world of sound. It may seem a simple thing to write for percussion; in reality, integrating it into the rest of the body of instrumental sound so it retains its identity, and amalgamating it with the sound of older instruments, requires much knowledge and subtlety. This "encyclopedia" of percussion will be an enormous help to performers and composers alike in achieving those objectives.

Pierre Boulez

ACKNOWLEDGMENTS

My thanks to all my professional colleagues who helped with my incessant queries, and to many manufacturers for their assistance with catalogues and photographs. And a huge "thank you" to my granddaughter Stephanie, for all the invaluable help she gave me with her computer skills and help in editing.

INTRODUCTION

The aim of this book is to show the world of percussion as it is today, at the dawn of the new millennium. The second half of the twentieth century saw tremendous development in all aspects of percussion, and though obviously there will always be change and development, I feel the percussion explosion of the last fifty years has now virtually come to an end—an ideal time for an assessment of where we are today and the changes that have occurred.

My first professional orchestra was the London Philharmonic, which I joined in 1956. In those far-off days, percussionists were expected to stand to play everything, even a single note, a practice that to me seemed rather bizarre. I always had a vision of the ensuing chaos if this expectation were to be extended to the wind and brass sections! Feeling fairly self-confident after two or three years, I decided that I would remain seated while playing the triangle part in Brahm's 4th Symphony. The reaction from the timpanist was one of total disgust and incredulity—this was a crime akin to high treason! There was still one conductor twenty years later who rued the day when percussionists ceased to stand!

My memories of the orchestra's percussion instruments are still engraved in my memory:

four hand-tuned timpani
three-octave C–C xylophone
two-and-a-half-octave glockenspiel (with raised screw heads as an added hazard!)
one-and-a-half-octave set of tubular bells (chimes)
two military (deep) snare drums, which rested on wooden trestles, i.e., at 45° playing angle, and *no* height adjustment!
40" single-headed bass drum
a "pair" of cymbals, 16" and 15", which rested on a chair in front—a suspended cymbal effect was achieved by holding the cymbal with one hand and the stick in the other
one tambourine with half the jingles missing
two triangles, which were mounted on large paper-clips to fasten on to the music stand—played with a 6" nail!
a tam-tam, approximately 28"—the sound always reminded me of kicking a dustbin/garbage pail!
a very inferior set of stick castanets

This meant that there was no hardware at all—not a single stand. How different from today, when to use twenty stands in one concert is considered in no way unusual. But the instruments themselves are but one indicator of the change: the technical demands on the percussionist have also grown quite dramatically. One reads with some amusement and disbelief that the first performance of Bartók's *Sonata for Two Pianos and Percussion* in 1938 apparently needed nearly forty rehearsals. Pierre Boulez's *Le Marteau sans maître* was widely considered unplayable when it was first published in the 1950s (not the first, nor the last, work to be so described), Boulez and his *Pli selon Pli*, for which the keyboard percussion parts were given a total of twenty rehearsals—sectional and orchestral—with the BBC Symphony in 1969, was given just eight rehearsals twenty years later. And of course the multiple percussion parts—the idea of a composer writing for marimba, xylophone, vibraphone, crotales, bass drum, tam-tams, gongs, snare drum, and five tom-toms for *one player* would have been considered ludicrous in my college days—today it doesn't raise an eyebrow.

Another important change has been the vast improvement in percussion tuition. In my time at college, keyboard, voice, strings, woodwind, and brass were taken seriously by the authorities; other instruments, including guitar and percussion, were barely tolerated. Today, things are very different, and the number of percussion students eager to enter music college has never been higher. There is now also the Percussive Arts Society, originating in the United States, but now with chapters around the world for all with an interest in percussion.

The final key to the advancement of percussion has been the influence of pop music, jazz, and film scores, not forgetting, of course, that as travel and communication have become so much easier composers have become much more aware of the distinctive timbres of a seemingly endless variety of ethnic percussion instruments. The breaking down of the barriers which once separated so-called serious music from the jazz and pop fields has also been crucial. As a student I would have been thrown out immediately if it had been known that I was also secretly taking kit lessons, but such days—when, for example, a (now very eminent) guitarist was told to get out of the Royal College of Music in

London with that infernal instrument—are long past. I have always found it strange that one wasn't supposed to be able to enjoy the legends of the jazz world or some of the pop icons as well as Beethoven, Mahler, or Stravinsky: today a catholicity of taste is regarded as quite normal—there is only good music and bad music. Or, as I heard a famous singer put it recently, "I just enjoy music—I don't recognize any boundaries."

My forty-five years as a percussionist on the London musical scene have brought me into contact with many of the world's top conductors and composers, and I have taken part in a large number of first performances and film scores. Much of this has been a great privilege, and all of it has, naturally, shaped my ideas on percussion, percussion writing, and playing (not to mention conductors and composers). This book therefore, in addition to offering factual information, reflects my own deeply held views of percussion as it is today, at the dawn of the new millennium—for the composer,

arranger, and percussionist a truly astonishing range of sound is available, with unending subtleties of timbre and colour.

When reading the following section of this book, *The Instruments*, note that many of these percussion instruments are accompanied by a photo. Some also come with a definition of the instrument's range, as shown by the following:

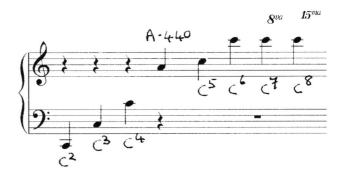

THE INSTRUMENTS

My music dictionary when I was at college in the early 1950s listed just nineteen percussion instruments, including celeste and dulcitone. It contains entries that today appear extraordinary, such as "marimba—a sort of xylophone, it appears to be taken seriously in the United States, and Percy Grainger has included it in one or two works," or "bass drum . . . can be quietly awe-inspiring, but at times may descend to mere carpet beating." Also, "tubular bells . . . usually in the diatonic scale of E♭, but occasionally a chromatic scale—thus actual tunes can be played if desired." Even more puzzling is an entry entitled "Marimba Gongs": "they are something like the marimba, but with metal bars instead of wood, so resembling the glockenspiel or celeste." Reading items such as these in a respected dictionary now seems laughable—even farcical—given the changes of the last fifty years.

We have now progressed to such an extent that in this book I can list around 250 instruments and effects. But percussion is now an extremely complicated subject, and inevitably there is much confusion, even amongst players—there are different understandings in different countries, and widely differing availabilities of instruments. Therefore we have to be a little patient with our composer and conductor colleagues. To list just two very minor examples: a tenor drum in Britain and America is taken to be an unsnared drum, but in most other countries it may be snared or unsnared; in the U.S. a vibraphone is taken to be a three-octave F–F instrument (a recent American percussion encyclopedia adds that "a few instruments have been custom-made in ranges of three and a half octaves, C–F, and four octaves, C–C"; but in Europe the four-octave instrument has been available from some manufacturers for many years, appearing in an Ajax (London) catalogue as early as the 1930s. Alban Berg wrote for it in his opera *Lulu*, also in the 1930s, and virtually all the Henze compositions require four octaves. An additional complication is that there are many percussion instruments that have an *element* of pitch. Some of these have also been developed chromatically, so that now they are sometimes pitched and sometimes unpitched, examples being blocks, rototoms, anvils, bottles, gongs, cowbells, and stones (lithophone). The instruments that have an element of pitch but are *not* found chromatically include triangles, cymbals, snare drums, tam-tams, and tambourines. However, the composer may still ask for a graduated series of sounds. But while so many new percussion instruments appeared in the last century, we have to acknowledge that others quietly faded away into near or sometimes total obscurity. This list would include the dulcimer, dulcitone, glass armonica, keyboard xylophone (*xilophono a tastiera*), lithophone, metallophone, musical saw, nabimba, and the five-octave xylomarimba. Of these, only the glass armonica shows any sign of a revival.

It is also impossible to be precise about many percussion instruments. Every violin has the same G, D, A, and E strings and every B♭ clarinet has the same range; in percussion it is very different, and the reader will notice frequent use of words such as *usually*, *about*, or *sometimes*. A perfect case in point is the range of the keyboard instruments: there are frequently four or five different sizes of marimba in the same catalogue; in a multiple percussion set-up, to be presented with a larger instrument than necessary may be inconvenient, or even possibly make the part unplayable—to have an extra two-foot length of instrument when it is not needed can be *very* frustrating!

In addition, there are instruments that occasionally appear in percussion parts or scores that are not legitimately part of a percussionist's skills, though there are usually some players who have studied them. This includes instruments such as celeste, cimbalom, and glass armonica, and these are all included in the instrument list here. There are also instruments or effects designed by composers to meet the requirements of particular works. Sometimes these find their way into mainstream percussion; others remain hidden away waiting for the next performance.

A relatively new development is the confusion caused by manufacturers imitating ethnic instruments but giving them new names. Confusion is also caused by the many slight variations in spelling, especially of African instruments.

Finally, with such a vast range of instruments now available, the percussionist has come to expect composers and conductors to ask for a "drier" tambourine sound, or a darker cymbal, a different type of bass drum or a larger tam-tam—we are very largely victims of our own success. (Though, strangely, I've never heard a conductor ask for a larger cello, or a smaller bass clarinet!)

The availability of some percussion instruments and accessories varies tremendously from country to country, and I have therefore included names of some of the most important manufacturers and suppliers with their current range of instruments, accessories, percussion music, literature, and so on. Information about these individual companies can be found in the Percussion Manufacturers and Suppliers chapter later in the book.

A

Affolants

Appears mainly in some works by Iannis Xenakis. A suspended sheet of thin metal, giving a very bright, ethereal sound (e.g., Xenakis's *Persephassa*, for six percussionists).

Afuche *see* Cabaca

Agogo Bells

A Brazilian instrument from the samba bands consisting of two (usually) small cone-shaped bells on a sprung steel hoop (see figure). The player holds the instrument in one hand and a wooden or metal stick in the other (although agogo bells are most often mounted in Western orchestras). A variety of sounds and rhythmic patterns are produced by sriking the bell(s) in different spots and squeezing the bells closer together. There are now also variations on the original, in the form of triple and quattro agogos, and a blade agogo—a small metal blade between the two bells. There are also wooden agogos—in this case the "bells" are side by side and not on a sprung steel hoop.

P.J. Percussion

Agogo Bell Tree

A graduated series of around nine agogo bells facilitating a glissando effect. Available from PJ Drums and Percussion.

See also Ghana Bell

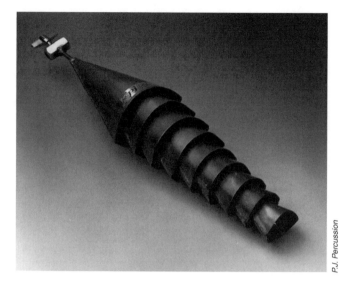

P.J. Percussion

Almglocken *see* Cowbells

Ankle Bells

A strap with a number of tiny bells worn around a dancer's ankle. Also sometimes worn on the dancer's wrist. Available from AfroTon, Asian Sound, PJ Drums and Percussion, World Beat Percussion, and others.

AfroTon

Anklung

An instrument from Indonesia and Java, consisting of split tubes of bamboo loosely attached to a frame. When shaken they produce a dry-pitched rattling sound—each note is two tubes tuned in octaves. They are obviously not in chromatic form in their original environment, but are now increasingly used that way in Western music; their usual range is around two octaves. Takemitsu uses a single note for four of the five solo percussionists in *From Me Flows What You Call Time*. Available from AfroTon and Kolberg, who have three octaves, B^3–C^7.

Note: In East Java, "anklung" can sometimes mean similarly shaped bamboo tubes played xylophone style.

Antique Cymbals *see* Crotales; Finger Cymbals

Anvil

Fr. *enclume*; Ger. *Amboß*; It. *incudine*; Sp. *yunque*

The sound required is that of a blacksmith's anvil—a very high-pitched and penetrating metallic ring. The genuine article is used relatively rarely because of its great weight, and then usually for the additional visual effect rather than any vastly superior tone quality. The substitutes most frequently used are lengths of steel tube or pieces of railway line—any metal, in fact, that will give a realistic anvil sound.

Wagner scored for eighteen anvils in *Das Rheingold* (three sets of three high, two medium, and one low), and Verdi used three in the famous Anvil Chorus in *Il Trovatore*. In contemporary writing, George Benjamin writes for a sequence of twelve different-pitch steel tubes in *Antara*. In normal usage, of course, the anvil is of indefinite pitch, but Kolberg Percussion now additionally produces a two-octave set, C^3–C^5 (see figure below). As the sound is *so* penetrating, the wearing of earplugs when playing works such as *Das Rheingold* is strongly recommended.

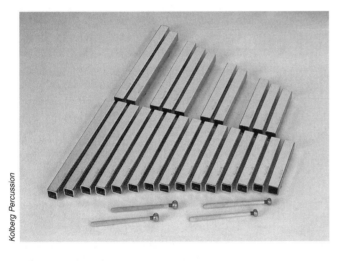

Kolberg Percussion

Apito *or* Samba Whistle

A wooden or, more usually now, metal whistle played by the leader of a Brazilian samba band. The apito has three pitches

P.J. Percussion

available for the leader to indicate instructions to the other players. The sound is very piercing and high-pitched. Apitos are widely available.

B

Balafon

The balafon is a native African xylophone, originating in Ghana, Guinea, and Senegal. Calabash gourds are used as resonators, and the instrument is tuned to an African scale with up to about twenty notes in the single row. The genuine balafon is available from Kambala Percussion in Austria and Sabar Roots Percussion and Afro Ton in Germany—the Marimba One instrument is modelled on the Shona balafons of Zimbabwe.

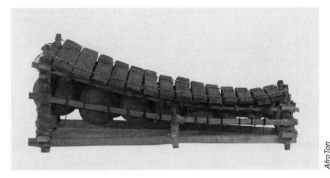

AfroTon

Baroque Timpani

As the name implies, timpani used for works of the Baroque period. By definition these are hand-tuned instruments with copper shells of calf heads. The diameter of the drums is somewhat smaller than those manufactured today, a pair of drums normally having diameters of around 19" and 22", up to about 22" and 24", and the shells will be hand-beaten. The genuine period instruments are still to be found, but Lefima appears to be the only manufacturer currently with Baroque timpani in their catalogue. Additionally, both Kolberg and Potter & Co. make them to order.

See also Timpani

Basler Trommel *or* Basle Drum

The Basler Trommel is a parade snare drum with the larger head diameter of around 16", and a similar depth. The shells used to be of wood, but are now normally of metal. The name comes from the Swiss city of Basle, and the drummers have developed a unique rudimentary technique. Its original use was in the drum and fife bands at carnival time, a tradition still very much in evidence today. Available from Giannini in Zurich and Lefima in Germany.

Bass Drum

Fr. *grosse caisse*; Ger. *grosse Trommel*; It. *gran cassa*; Sp. *bombo*

The origins of the bass drum are somewhat vague, though there is evidence of a drum of this type in ancient times, and it appears probable that it emanated from the Middle East. Today the bass drum is one of the fundamental percussion instruments, whether in an orchestra, a pop group, or a marching band. But although the name is the same, in reality it is three quite different instruments.

Kolberg Percussion

The bass drum in the orchestra

The orchestral bass drum comes in a variety of shapes and sizes, and there is a much wider acceptance today that different types of drum may be more suited to particular works. Huge variation in size is found, but for a symphony orchestra a drum of around 40" diameter and 16" depth is quite normal, and increasingly the drums are mounted on stands adjustable for angle—this makes life more comfortable for the player and also facilitates the playing of rhythmic passages timpani-style if desired. Some drums now have height adjustment as well. For the best tone quality the drum should be suspended by leather or rubber straps from a frame rather than being fixed, and similarly the adjustment for angle should be to the suspension frame rather than by a rod passing through the drum.

In Europe double-headed drums with a smaller head diameter but with very deep shells have long been popular, probably for historical reasons, with measurements of around a 32" head diameter and 26" depth. However, in Britain single-headed bass drums (sometimes called gong drums) were very much in vogue, and until around the 1960s were the norm in symphony orchestras. With the huge increase in recordings in the mid-twentieth century they became unpopular with some engineers and producers, as they can tend to have a more definite pitch, but they

are still ideal in certain situations. A very large single-headed drum of around 60" diameter can be used to great dramatic effect in the Dies Irae from Verdi's Requiem, and is even known as a "Verdi drum." However, a bass drum that would sound wonderful in a Mahler symphony would be totally inappropriate in Stravinsky's *Soldier's Tale,* for example. In other words, it is a case of matching the drum to the work.

The shell of the orchestral bass drum will be quite thick—for professional orchestras calf heads are virtually essential—and the pitch of the drum should be low and indefinable, the tone full and resonant. A wide range of mallets is required, and these must be of sufficient weight to draw out the full tone of the drum. Timpani or snare-drum sticks are generally totally unsuitable other than for a particular effect. In the hands of an expert the bass drum in the symphony orchestra is capable of great dramatic effect, Mahler's Third Symphony and Stravinsky's *Rite of Spring* being just two examples. Which type of drum and which sticks are used are generally left completely to the discretion of the player.

The pedal bass drum, as described below for pop and jazz use, also appears occasionally in the orchestra or the contemporary music ensemble. One of the first occasions was probably Milhaud's *Concert for Percussion and Orchestra*, written in 1929. Since the soloist also has four timpani in addition to several drums, cymbals, and effects, the problem is where to place a bass drum with pedal so that it is accessible without obstructing the other instruments; one solution available now is to use a small, single-headed pedal bass drum which takes up a minimal amount of space. John Adams's "The Chairman Dances" also requires pedal bass drum, as does the percussion soloist in James MacMillan's *Veni, Veni Emmanuel.*

Pop group and jazz use

In a jazz band, large or small, or a pop group, the bass drum is an essential part of the drum kit and again is played with a foot pedal. The shells of these bass drums are thinner, usually around a ¼" thick, of maple, birch, or other hardwood ply, and the heads will be of plastic. Again, the size of the drums may vary considerably according to taste, the *average* being around 20" diameter and 16" depth, rather smaller than the 28"-diameter drums that were so popular in the 1930s. The drum will have supporting legs or spurs either side at the front for stability, and the pedal clamps on to the counterhoop at the back. The pedal is also of primary importance, being balanced so that a very rapid succession of beats can be achieved. The beater is usually of wood or hard felt, according to the player's preference. The desired sound today is very low-pitched and dry, with no resonance whatsoever. Most players seated at a drumkit will use their right foot for the bass drum pedal and their left for the hi-hat, though some players prefer a set-up with two bass drums. The drummer's raison d'être is to provide the basic rhythmic drive underpinning the band or group and fill in as appropriate.

Bass drum in the marching band

The bass drummer in the marching band provides the main pulse both for the band and those marching behind. He sets and maintains the correct tempo, which in military bands may vary widely according to tradition. Again, the shells will usually be of a hardwood ply with a diameter of around 28" and depth of 12". As with the drumkit, bass drum plastic heads are now virtually universal, as is rod tensioning. The player strikes the drum in the centre with a hard felt beater producing a dry crack that will need to be heard at a considerable distance.

Bass drums, whether orchestral, marching band, or drumset, are available in every conceivable size and format from many manufacturers, large and small.

Bata Drum

Originating in Nigeria, bata drums came to Cuba during the years of the slave trade, and are now an established part of Latin American music. Originally the hourglass-shaped shells were of wood, the two heads tensioned by leather straps, and their use was in religious ceremonies. In contemporary terms they are more likely to be made of fibreglass and are rod-tensioned—one head is considerably larger than the other. There are three sizes: the iya is the largest, the middle drum is the itolel or omele, and the smallest the oconcolo. The measurements are likely to be roughly as follows:

iya	heads 12" and 7"	depth 29"
itolel	heads 9" and 6"	depth 26"
oconcolo	heads 7" and 5"	depth 22"

The player is normally seated, the left hand playing the higher-pitched head and the right hand the lower. The rhythms and playing technique are extremely complex. Available from LP, Meinl, and others.

Bells (*also* Chimes, Tubular Bells)

Fr. *cloches*; Ger. *Glocken, Röhrenglocken*; It. *campane*; Sp. *campanas*

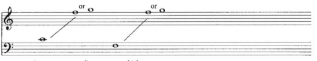

written range - sounding one octave higher

The bell is one of the oldest percussion instruments known, and there is evidence of its use in Asia 4,000 years ago. However, the word "bell" is used for many instruments, from tiny ankle bells, to cowbells, to fire bells, and on up to the massive cast bells found in cathedrals. In the orchestra the bell sound is most usually represented by sets of tubular bells, or chimes as they are known in the U.S., since the weight and size of conventional cast bells make them impractical for general use in a symphony orchestra. The earliest sets of tubular bells were in the diatonic scale of E♭, chromatic sets only appearing around the 1930s. One and half-octave sets with a written range from C^4 to F/G^5 (sounding one octave higher) have long been considered to be the norm, but two-octave sets, F^3–F/G^5, have been available in Europe since the 1960s and now Kolberg Percussion in Germany has manufactured a three-octave set, C^3–C^6. [Interestingly, Percy Grainger writes for two octaves plus, F^3–$A♭^5$, in *The Warriors*, written in 1922, and Charles Ives (1874–1954), who always wrote ambitious bell parts, wanted bells from $D♭^2$ to C^5 in *From the Steeples to the Mountains*.] Obviously the height of the two- and three-octave sets necessitates a built-in platform for the player if a continuous part is to be played. However, as the above demonstrates, the professional player will find that some composers have rather unrealistic ideas and write for bells below the bass clef and well beyond the treble clef. At either extremity overtones of tubular bells can be a problem. Because of their length—more than 5½' for the lowest bell even on the smaller one-and-a-half-octave

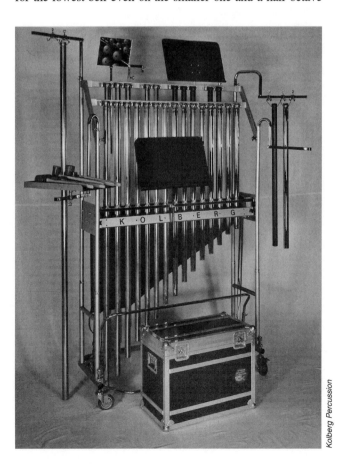

sets—reading a part of any complexity presents difficulties. The best option is to have the score in the centre above the bells, which will mean having a rostrum for the player and height extension on the pedal bar, which operates in similar fashion to the piano sustaining pedal. Rawhide or plastic hammers of some weight are needed to draw out the full tone, the hammer striking the top edge of the bell, which is usually capped. Sets of one-and half-octave bells in 1½" or 1¼" tube are made by Giannini, Ludwig Musser, Magestic, Premier, and Ufip; one-and-a-half-octave and two-octave sets by Adams, Bergerault, and Kolberg. Kolberg alone has made a three-octave set. Both Adams and Kolberg have additional fittings available for adding extra bells to the smaller sets. Percussion Plus in Britain has one-and-a-half-octave sets in 1" tube, which are ideal for schools and small orchestral work.

Cast Bells

Bell metal is an alloy of approximately 77 percent copper and 23 percent tin, and the tone quality of the cast bell is infinitely better than that of the tubular type. The size and weight of cast bells precludes their general use in the orchestra, but in my experience no attempt at re-creating their sound by sampling or other artificial means has come close to success in the concert hall. (In addition, the visual aspect in concert is a plus that cannot be ignored.) Some opera houses have cast bells available, the most notable being that of the Bolshoi in Moscow with three octaves. The largest cast bell ever made was also made in Russia, weighing an incredible 170 tons! But though they appear relatively rarely in the symphony orchestra at present, I have long felt that they will increasingly be used for certain works where only one or two notes are needed. This opinion has now been confirmed: I have heard of several orchestras, including the New York Philharmonic and the Royal Liverpool Philharmonic, purchasing their own bells (the Berlin Philharmonic have owned the C and G for the Berlioz *Symphonie fantastique* for many years). Other works that would benefit from the superior tone of the cast bell include Ravel's arrangement of Mussorgsky's *Pictures at an Exhibition* (low E♭), Richard Strauss's *Also Sprach Zarathustra* (low E), and Puccini's *Tosca* (F, B♭, and F). Shchedrin writes for five church bells, unspecified pitch, in *Stihira*, and five cast bells (B♭^{3}, A^4, F, B^5, and C^6) in *The Chimes: Concerto for Orchestra*. Webern writes for deep bells without definite pitch in *Five Pieces for Orchestra* (Op. 10), and *Six Pieces for Orchestra* (Op. 6). I certainly envisage percussion rental companies in the not-too-distant future having two or three octaves of cast bells available. There are few bell foundries left in existence today; two of the oldest must be the Whitechapel Bell Foundry in London, which has its originals in 1420, and Petit & Fritsen in Holland, established back in 1660.

Bell Lyra

Bell lyra is the name given to the glockenspiel used in marching bands, arranged pyramid fashion on a pole, played with one hand, the other holding the pole. However, the bell lyra is increasingly being superseded by a conventional glockenspiel, but with a shoulder harness, so that the instrument is in the normal playing position and the player can freely use both hands. The usual range is two octaves, C^5–C^7, or sometimes two and a half octaves, G^4–C^7. Both types are available from most companies with marching-band percussion in their catalogue—see the Percussion Manufacturers and Suppliers chapter later in the book.

See also Glockenspiel.

Bell Plates

Fr. *cloches-plaques*; Ger. *Plattenglocken*; It. *campane in lastra di metallo*

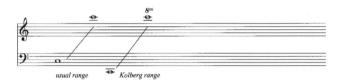

usual range   Kolberg range

Bell plates are rectangular metal plates with a bell-like sound. Though emanating from Asia they were developed in Europe in the second half of the twentieth century and are increasingly used in contemporary music. The most usual available range is three octaves (C^3–C^6), but Kolberg Percussion in Germany produces five octaves (C^2–C^7). Though now marketed by various companies, the weight and therefore the tone quality can vary considerably, but at their best they are a viable substitute for a number of cast bells. However, using several octaves of bell plates does present problems: (1) because of the distance involved (a single C^2 plate is around 35" × 25") the bottom *half*-octave of the Kolberg plates uses approximately the same space as the top *two* octaves; (2) simultaneous damping of a number of plates is impossible for one player (the sound decay is very long); (3) there may also be problems for the player having a consistent view of the conductor; and (4) as with some other chromatic percussion, the heavy mallets necessary for the bottom notes will be totally unsuitable for the high notes, that is, as with Messiaen parts for Almglocken (tuned cowbells), two or three players may be needed for the full range. Boulez writes for two octaves of bell plates in *Pli selon pli*, and Holliger similarly in *Siebengesang*. In addition to Kolberg, bell plates are also available from Adams and Ufip.

Kolberg Percussion

Bell Tree (*also known as* Chinese Bell Tree)

The standard bell tree consists of a number of small, cup-shaped bells (usually around twenty-five to thirty), of different pitch suspended in order of size on a cord or rod. When a light metal beater is passed across the bells a shimmering glissando effect is produced. There is also now a hand-held bell tree, which has a similar effect and is about half the size, i.e., with around fourteen bells. An alternative effect is achieved with bell trees with only five or six lower-pitched bells. Bell trees are widely available, PJ Drums and Percussion in particular having several versions. (A Turkish crescent or Jingling Johnny is also sometimes mistakenly called a bell tree.)

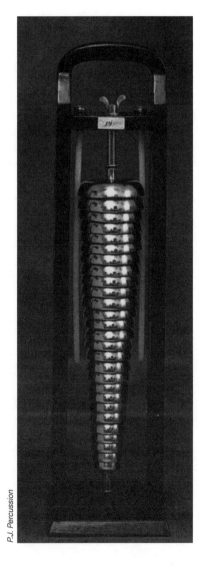

P.J. Percussion

Berimbau

A wooden bow (standing) usually around 6' long with an attached gourd. It has a metal string, caxixi rattle, metal ring, and beater, and pressure on the bow changes the pitch. The gourd is attached to the string about one-third of the way up, and forms a resonating chamber. The player

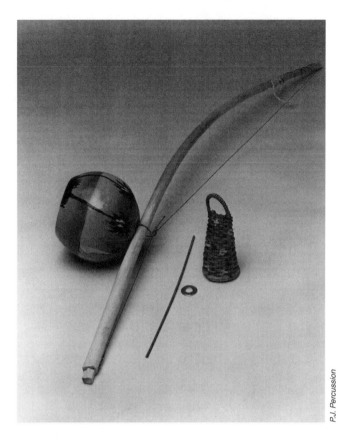

P.J. Percussion

holds the metal washer in the left hand and small wooden stick and caxixi rattle in the right. Originally developed from a hunting bow, this is another African instrument now mostly appearing in the Latin American bands. It is widely available.

See also Caxixis

Bhaya *see* Tabla

Bicycle Bell

Literally the type of bell found on a child's bicycle, with the thumb activating a lever so that a tiny hammer strikes the high-pitched bell several times in quick succession. Giordano wrote for this in his opera *Fedora* (1898)—also probably the first opera to require bicycles on stage!

Binsasara (*also known as* Kokiriko)

A Japanese effect consisting of a large number of very small rectangular wooden boards strung together on a rope with a handle at each end. A sharp shake of the hand produces a ripple effect as sixty to eighty boards consecutively strike one another in very rapid succession, giving a sharp guttural *crrrrack*. Available from Asian Sound, Kolberg Percussion LP, Meinl, and World Beat Percussion (the last three use the name kokiriko).

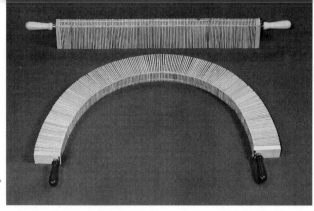

Kolberg Percussion

Birds

Thirty to forty small fibreglass shells strung together; when these are shaken the sound is of a flock of twittering birds. Marketed by Meinl.

Bodhran (pronounced *bough-rawn*)

The bodhran is a single-headed Irish frame drum of around 18" diameter, sometimes found with jingles inset in the rim, but most usually without. A wooden beater shaped at both ends plays the intricate rhythms for Irish folk-dancing, the beater being held in the centre and the player's wrist oscillating back and forth. Apart from holding the drum, the other hand also damps the sound when required, helping to complement the musical phrase. Bodhrans are now widely available. Serious students can refer to Micheal O'Suilleabhain, *The Bodhran*, published by Waltons Musical Instrument Galleries, 2–5, North Frederick Street, Dublin I, Eire—an easy-to-learn method book showing the different regional styles and techniques.

Bones

Pairs of flat bones or wooden slats about 6"–8" long are held in one hand between the thumb and first and second fingers. When the wrist is turned quickly the bones strike each other with a dry, clacking sound. The wrist action is similar to that required for the bodhran.

Bongos

Bongos are the highest-pitched hand drums, originating in the Latin American bands but now appearing in all types of music. Pairs of single-headed drums are of around 6" and 8" diameter, with a depth of around 7". The counterhoop strains the skin over the shell and is well below the level of the head. The player is normally seated, and holds the drums between the knees with the larger drum on the right. The sound is high-pitched, fairly dry, and penetrating. In the hands of an expert a wide spectrum of sounds is possible, fingers and hands being used to produce a variety of open, ringing sounds as well as muffled strokes. The interpretation is left entirely to the player's imagination and musicality. Bongos are now widely used in all types of music, though in the symphony orchestra they are more likely to be used as high tom-toms, mounted on a stand and played with sticks. The real bongo sound is essentially that of the hand-played instrument. Available universally.

See also Clay Bongo

Boobams

usual written range - sounding two octaves higher

Boobams came into being as lengths of bamboo, one end being covered with vellum or skin. This has now been developed into a chromatic sequence of drums, and somewhere along the way the name was transposed into boobam. The diameter of the head, around 4½", is constant throughout the range, the difference in pitch being controlled by the length of the resonators. Plastic heads are now virtually universal, and the player uses fingers or softish mallets. The sound is quite distinctive, perhaps best described as a cross between a marimba and single-headed tom-toms. Although not produced by the main percussion manufacturers, they are available from specialist companies. The usual range is two octaves, F^3–F^5, but Kolberg offer three octaves, C^3–C^6. Henze uses two octaves of boobams in *Tristan* and one octave in *Voices*.

See also Octobans

Kolberg Percussion

Bougarabou

The bougarabou is an African hand drum somewhat similar to the congas of the Latin American bands. It has a hand-carved wooden body from a single trunk and a cowskin head with rope tensioning. The bass sound is somewhat warmer than that of the conga. Available in several sizes from AfroTon, Kambala Percussion, and Sabar Roots Percussion.

AfroTon

Bouteillephone

Fr. *bouteillephone*; Ger. *Flaschenspiel*; It. *il suono die bottiglia*

The bouteillephone is a series of tuned bottles forming a chromatic range. As with wineglasses they can be tuned to a degree by adding water. Kolberg produce three octaves,

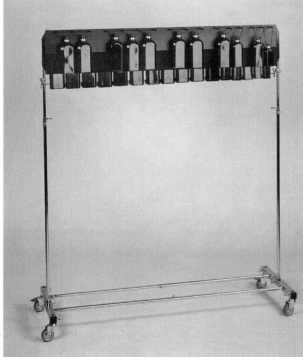

Kolberg Percussion

C^4–D^7. Probably the most famous example of orchestral use of the bouteillephone is still Erik Satie's Parade, requiring two octaves D^5–D^7—quite difficult to play at the written tempo, but a great effect when mastered.

Brake Drums

One of a number of effects borrowed from the automobile, the upturned steel brake drum has a high-pitched, clear metallic ring when struck with a heavy metal beater or hammer. Different sizes of brake drum obviously produce a variety of pitches, and the effect has been used by a number of composers. They are mostly obtainable from scrapyards, but the Kolberg catalogue has four different sizes available.

Kolberg Percussion

Bugarabou *see* Bougarabou

Bull Roarer (*also known as* Thunderstick)

The bull roarer is known with some tribes in Africa and with the Aborigines in Australia. It is a slim, shaped, flat piece of wood with designs engraved on both surfaces. One end is attached to a cord several feet long, and when whirled around at speed it produces the sound from which comes the name. The player thus needs quite a lot of space, which can present problems on a concert platform or in a recording studio (I remember three being used simultaneously during a film session on one occasion), especially if the player has a large

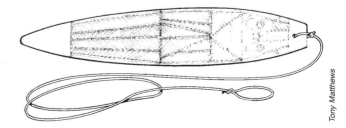

Tony Matthews

number of other instruments. The bull-roarer appears in the AfroTon catalogue, but otherwise may be difficult to find, apart from in tourist shops or in Australia.

Burano (*also known as* Devil Chaser)

A bamboo stick around 15" long, split down the middle from one end to a depth of 7"–8". When struck together the two tongues briefly vibrate together.

Burma Bell (*also known as* Kyisi *and* Thai Plate Bell)

A small, flat, brass plate bell, shaped like a Pagoda, with a clear, high-pitched tone. It is suspended by a cord, and a vibrato is obtained by striking the bell in the corner, so that it spins after the impact. Available in several sizes, from around 6"–12", from Kolberg and Asian Sound in Germany and Ufip in Italy.

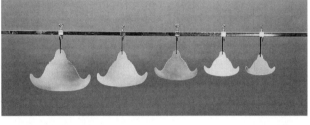

Kolberg Percussion

Buzz Marimba *see* Nabimba

C

Cabaca *or* Afuche

A Latin American instrument, this consists of a gourd, usually a coconut shell, with small ridges carved into the surface and a handle added. The gourd is encased in a loose mesh of

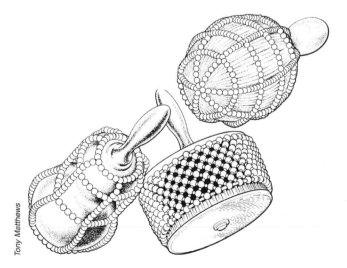

Tony Matthews

beads. The player holds the mesh against the shell with one hand and twists the handle with the other, producing a dry, gravelly sound. There are now also many imitations by Western manufacturers, one (initially from LP) being of special note—a wooden cylinder encased in a serrated metal surface: the beads in this case are replaced by a series of chains made up of tiny ball-bearings. The sound is probably higher-pitched and more abrasive than that of the natural gourd. Cabacas are now widely used in all types of music, and are widely available. The sound of the cabaca is quite similar to the Nigerian shekere, though probably higher in pitch.
See also Shekere

Caixa *see* Tarol

Cajon (pronounced *cah-hone*)

The Cajon was originally a Latin America hand drum with a wooden playing surface. After the repression of the years of the slave trade, the cajon had evolved to a simple wooden box construction, and in contemporary terms is an essential rhythm instrument in flamenco music. Available from Schlagwerk Percussion, Worldbeat Percussion, and others.

Campanelli Giapponese

Campanelli giapponese is an effect specifically designed for Puccini's *Madame Butterfly* and consists of four metal bars, tuned to C^4, E^4, C^5, and E^5, suspended over resonators. Available from Kolberg.

Chalklin Percussion

Car Horns

Fr. *klaxon, trompe d'auto*; Ger. *Autohupe*; It. *clacson*

Car horns are an effect occasionally called for by composers, not the modern version of course, but the bulb-type

Kolberg Percussion

motor horns found on the early automobiles. Gershwin famously used four horns pitched in A, B, C, and D in *An American in Paris*, and Ligeti used a series of twelve (unpitched), in his original version of *Le Grand Macabre*, each of the three players having four horns, one for each hand and foot. Poulenc uses high and low motor horns in *The Story of Babar the Little Elephant*. Apart from the sets of A, B, C, and D for the Gershwin, Kolberg produce two octaves, C^3–C^5, as do Deutsche Signal Instrumenten-Fabrik.

Castanets

Fr. *castagnettes*; Ger. *Kastagnetten*; It. *nacchere*; Sp. *castanuelas*

Castanets are traditionally one of the oldest percussion effects, and are of course indelibly linked with Spain, where together with the guitar they almost have the status of a national instrument. Derived from the ancient eastern finger cymbals, castanets are a pair of slightly hollowed shells, usually of walnut, ebony, or rosewood, connected at the top by a cord. Originally used by dancers, the cord is looped over the thumb leaving the fingers free to click the castanets together. Usually the male, or lower-pitched, castanet is held in the left hand, the female, the higher-pitched, in the right. A trill is achieved by a continuous four-beat pattern: one click of the left-hand castanet, followed by a succession of three clicks by the fingers of the right hand. Some flamenco dancers use a technique in which the castanet is looped over the middle finger of each hand. While this obviously alters the finger pattern, the basic approach is similar.

In the symphony orchestra of course, playing demands are quite different, though for some of the core repertoire such as de Falla's *Three-Cornered Hat* it is a great advantage if one member of the percussion section has mastered the traditional technique. However, at other times it is just impractical, given the fact that it takes a few seconds to loop

the castanets over the thumbs. This has led to other options being available to the orchestral percussionist:

1. *The castanet machine*, where two pairs of castanets are mounted side by side on a wooden block, or where the block has two hollowed-out circles with a single castanet over each. In both cases these castanets are mounted, and tensioned by springs or elastic. The sound quality is of course slightly inferior, and only an open-type roll is available—a poor imitation of the real thing.
2. *Stick or handle castanets*. A wooden stick with one end shaped and hollowed out and a castanet to strike each side. A more sophisticated version of this dispenses with the shaped end and substitutes only a small metal tongue between the castanets: the bottom of each castanet shell is slightly chamfered to facilitate the playing of rhythms with a genuine castanet sound. This very superior model was introduced by Frank Epstein in the U.S.

Castanets of all types are widely available.
See also Metal Castanets

Catuba

The word *catuba* sometimes appears in Rossini opera scores; it is not an instrument as such—the letters stand for CAssa TUrkish BAnda. The composer's exact ideas on this are of course now somewhat difficult to guess: the nearest interpretation today appears to be any combination of bass drum, cymbals, triangle, etc., in accordance with the wishes of the conductor!

Caxixis

Caxixis are small woven Brazilian basket rattles. Traditionally they have a wooden base, but increasingly Western manufacturers use a base of fibreglass or metal to produce a rather sharper sound. Caxixis are also traditionally used with the berimbau, the player using one hand to hold the caxixis together with the thin stick that strikes the wire. They are widely available.

Celeste

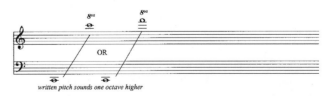

written pitch sounds one octave higher

The celeste was invented in Paris in 1886 by Mustel. It has steel bars, each with its own wooden box resonator, and a piano-type keyboard operates the felt-covered hammers; there is also a sustaining pedal. Though visually similar to the keyed glockenspiel, the celeste has a gentle, soft, rounded tone.

Kolberg Percussion

Ranges vary, but five or five and a half octaves are now usual for a symphony orchestra. Notation is as for the piano, over two staves, but the celeste sounds one octave higher than written. Though the celeste is seen as a percussion instrument in the strictest sense, it should *not* be regarded as part of the percussion section, and in the symphony orchestra is normally played by a keyboard player, not a percussionist. Including the celeste in percussion scores can give players, librarians, and conductors many unnecessary problems. (Additionally, keyboard players are naturally concerned at any encroachment on their territory!) Principal manufacturers are Schiedmayer and Kolberg in Germany, and Yamaha in Japan.

Cencerros *see* Cowbells

Chains

Fr. *la chaine*; Ger. *die Kettenrassel*; It. *la catena*

Chains are seldom found in the symphony orchestra, but do appear at times with great effect, as in Schoenberg's Gurrelieder. As with some other percussion instruments, the name itself is somewhat imprecise—a chain can be a tiny necklace at one extreme, to the huge links of a chain for a ship's anchor at the other. Mostly, as for *Gurrelieder* and Janáček's opera *House of the Dead*, a medium-heavy type is needed. The player must remember to drop them as he finishes a passage, or he may be left holding the chains in mid-air, with the prospect of the slightest involuntary movement producing a loud, unwanted clink! Henze uses chains on a timpani, a cymbal, and a metal plate in his Sixth Symphony—obviously a rather lighter type in this instance. George Crumb writes for heavy iron chains in *Star Child*.

Another, very different, use that may be required is sliding a small chain across the edge of a gong or tam-tam.

Chimes (American terminology for tubular bells) *see* Bells

Chinese Cymbal *see* Cymbals

Chinese Opera Gong

Chinese opera gongs are of very small diameter, usually around 8"–10", but with a very distinctive sound quality: when they are struck, the initial impact sound is followed by a sharp rise or fall in pitch. Some gongs have the upward glissando, some the downward. Visually it is impossible to differentiate between the two. Available from Asian Sound, Wu Han-Chinalight, and Yuet Wah Music.

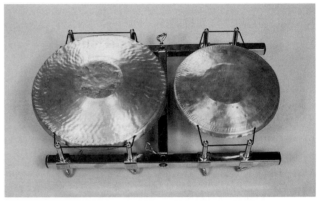

Kolberg Percussion

Chinese Tom-Tom

Chinese tom-toms were widely used in the jazz kits of the early twentieth century. The drums have a slightly convex wooden shell, the thick skin or vellum is nailed on, and they are frequently brightly decorated, often with dragons. They

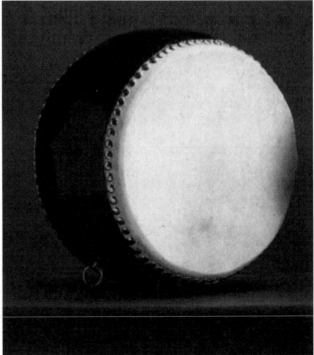

Asian Sound

were originally suspended from rings either side of the shell. The most usual sizes have a head diameter of between 10" and 20" and a depth of around 6"–10". The sound is very distinctive, being rather flatter and darker than the conventional tom-tom. Robert Gerhard was one composer who used these instruments to great effect. Appearing rather less frequently are the larger Chinese tom-toms, which may also have a greater shell depth, or even be free-standing. Chinese tom-toms can now be difficult to find in the West apart from Asian Sound in Cologne. However, Yuet Wah in Hong Kong has all the Chinese percussion instruments.

Ching Ching *see* Cymbals

Ching Ring (*also known as a* Hi-Hat Sock Jingle)

A circular metal frame of around 6" diameter with tambourine jingles around the edge, designed to fit on top of a hi-hat, usually for adding a rock tambourine sound. Available from Universal Percussion and others.

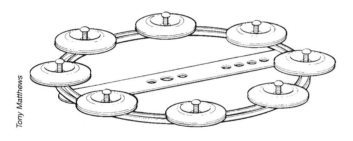

Tony Matthews

Chocola *or* Chocalho

Fr. *chocaoho-tubo*; Ger. *Schlittelrohr*; It. *tubo*; Sp. *chocalho*

The chocola is a Brazilian metal tube shaker containing beads or pellets, used in samba bands but now appearing in all types of music. The ganza is seemingly identical. The tube is usu-

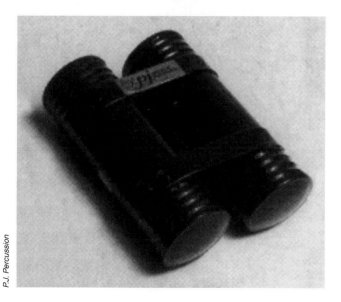

P.J. Percussion

ally around 2" in diameter, and may be from 6" to 18" in length. There are also versions with two or three tubes parallel to one another, and fibreglass ganzas enclosed in a rattan basket. Boulez uses a variety of these shakes in *Rituel: In memoriam Bruno Maderna*. All types are widely available.

Cimbalom

The cimbalom is another instrument that, strictly speaking, is percussion but in practice is not normally regarded as such. However, it does appear that an increasing number of percussionists are learning the instrument, and in Britain I can think of at least five or six who are also very accomplished on the cimbalom. In the early 1970s the situation was very different, with concert performers of adequate ability very difficult to find. This dearth of players led Pierre Boulez to commission the making of a cimbalom in a totally different format, with the strings laid out in normal keyboard pattern so that any percussion player could treat it as just another tuned percussion instrument. However, the tone quality was completely inadequate, and the instrument was written off as a failed experiment. (Additionally, it would have been a nightmare to play as a mallet instrument, with the strings being the equivalent of bars a mere ⅜" wide!) Just as castanets are associated with Spain, the cimbalom is essentially East European, and is from Hungary in particular, where it is a cornerstone of the Magyar gypsy band, the player having great freedom to extemporize. The cimbalom is a direct descendant of the santur of the Middle East. The standard cimbalom (the Hungarian word for dulcimer) has a four-octave E–E range with an extra D at the bottom, but it appears that most concert players opt for an extended range down to C^2 at the bottom, and up to A^6 at the top. The strings pass laterally across the layer with two, three, or four strings to each note according to the register. The sticks used are around 12" in length, with a curved end, which usually has a covering of wool or felt. Obviously, different coverings provide the player with a wide choice of timbre, and for a really brittle tone the stick will have no covering at all. Until the early nineteenth century the cimbalom was a portable instrument, rather smaller than today, and was played on the knees or suspended by a strap around the player's neck. As it developed, the problem of damping the strings became more urgent, and after various systems had been tried, the instrument-maker Schunda of Budapest introduced the damper pedal that is most commonly found today. The popularity of the cimbalom increased tremendously in the nineteenth century, and Schunda alone apparently made over six thousand instruments between 1874–98.

Chris Bradley

The cimbalom has a wonderfully distinctive tone, and orchestrally has attracted not only Hungarian composers such as Bartók, Kodály, and Kurtag, but also Stravinsky (*Renard, Ragtime, Les Noces*),* Boulez (*Éclat*) and Birtwistle (*Gawain*). Orchestrally, the most famous example is probably still Kodály's *Háry János*. It is worthy of note that the cimbalom virtuoso Aladar Racz (1886–1958) was dubbed the "Liszt of the cimbalom" by Saint-Saëns, and he later met Stravinsky in Geneva, who acquired an instrument from Racz, studied the technique, and then played daily for some twenty years.

A notable maker of these instruments is Istvan Jancso, with the company Kozmoaz Ipari. That company and the World Cimbalom Association can be found at Kozmosz Kultürcikk és Fémárukat Gyártó, Ipari Szövetkezet, 1065 Budapest, Hajos u. 25, Hungary; tel. 36–312–4211; fax 36–312–0831; e-mail: kozmosz@matavnet.hu.

See also Dulcimer

*The *Les Noces* that we are all familiar with today was Stravinsky's third and definitive version. The first was written in 1917, and employed a fairly full orchestra plus cimbalom; the second, from 1919, uses a pianola, harmonium, percussion, and two cimbaloms; the final version of 1922 uses four pianos plus percussion, including timpani and xylophone.

Claves

Claves are pairs of round, hardwood sticks, usually of rosewood or ebony, around 7½" long and 1¼" in diameter, and are an integral part of Latin American music. One hand is cupped with a clave resting over, being held very lightly between the fingertips and thumb: the other clave is held at one end and strikes the resonating clave in the centre. The distinctive, high-pitched sound will cut through the thickest orchestration. Though thought of as unpitched, there is in fact an element of pitch, and of course both the pitch and quality of sound will vary with the size and type of the claves.

In the symphony orchestra claves now appear frequently; if they are used in multiple percussion set-ups it is sometimes necessary for one clave to be placed on a stand or frame so that it can be played with xylophone mallets, though of course this does detract from the sound quality.

Rather more unusual are metal claves, used by James Wood in *Oreion* and Peter Maxwell Davies in *Revelation and Fall*.

Clay Bongo

As indicated by the name, these are bongos made of clay, but the similarity to real bongos is only slight. The clay bongos are from Morocco, and are rather smaller in head diameter, thus being higher in pitch; also, of course, the heads are laced and therefore not tensionable. Obviously the construction is nowhere near as robust as that of conventional bongos.

Coconut Shells

The shell of a coconut is split in two, and when drummed on the floor or a board will produce a fairly realistic sound of galloping horses. Hardwood shells are also produced for this effect.

Concert Toms

Concert toms are sets of tom-toms, usually single-headed, and available usually in sets of six or eight. Head diameters are from 6" to about 16" or 18". They are mounted two to a stand that is adjustable for angle as well as height. Concert toms are now the usual first choice for the tom-tom sound in the orchestra. The smaller drums pack down into the two largest for travelling purposes. Available from Kolberg, Ludwig Musser, Majestic, Remo, and Vancore.

Kolberg Percussion

Conch Shell

The conch shell, or shell trumpet, is the shell of a large ocean mollusk. The tip or the side is cut off to leave a hole for blowing. The fundamental mystical cooing sound is usually pitched around the bottom of the treble clef, and can be quite resonant. The effect is used but rarely, the one example in my experience being John Cage's *Third Construction*. Available from AfroTon.

AfroTon

Concussion Blocks *see* Hyoshigi

Congas (*also known as* Tumbas)

Congas are the largest hand drums in Afro-Cuban percussion, normally used in sets of two, three, or sometimes four.

P.J. Percussion

The head diameters vary slightly, but are approximately 10" for the highest drum, the nino or requinto, 11" for the quinto, 12" for the conga, and 13" for the tumba or tumbadora. The shells are barrel-shaped and have a depth of about 30". Originally, the barrel-making technique was used: long strips of wood were glued and clamped together; today the shells are probably more likely to be of fibreglass, which is claimed to give more sound projection. Thick rawhide heads are essential, tightly tensioned, and the player uses a combination of cupped hand, slaps, and finger strokes—the sound is full and very resonant. The drums are usually mounted, and are now widely used in all types of music. When they are used orchestrally, vibraphone or timpani mallets are frequently employed, obviously changing the sound quality. Available universally.

Congitas

Congitas are miniature congas, made in pairs, and are a fairly recent attempt to recreate the volume and tone of the conga, but with the attack and bite of bongos. Head diameters are most usually about 8–9", but may be as large as 10–12". Available from Meinl, Remo, and others.

Cowbells *or* Almglocken

Fr. *cloche de vache*; Ger. *Almglocken, Kuhglocken, Herdenglocken*; It. *campanaccio*; Sp. *cencerro*

As the names implies, cowbells originally had a clapper swinging loosely inside, and were hung around the necks of cattle so that they could be located easily in the large areas of grazing. In percussion terms they are two quite different instruments, though both of course are without the clapper.

1. Closer to the original, these have more of a rounded shape and have been developed chromatically into a four-octave range, F^3–F^7. Messiaen popularized them more than any other composer, and their tone quality is heard to great effect in works such as *Et exspecto resurrectionem mortuorum, Sept hai kai*, and *Couleurs de la Cité Céleste*. In *Et exspecto* three players are required for the cowbells, and of course rather softer, heavier mallets are needed for the bottom register. They have also been used as an unpitched effect in Mahler's Sixth Symphony and Webern's *Five Pieces for Orchestra*.

2. In much more general use is the modern cowbell, an essential element in Latin American percussion. In this context it is a straight-sided cowbell, sometimes used as a hand-held instrument, sometimes mounted. The

Kolberg Percussion

sound is less bell-like and rather drier. A very wide variety of sizes and timbres is available. The straight-sided Latin-type cowbell is widely available from many manufacturers. The chromatic cowbells are only available from specialist companies such as Kolberg (four octaves, F^3–F^7) and Asian Sound.

Crash Cymbals *see* Cymbals

Crasher *or* Effector

A crasher is three or four metal plates loosely riveted together, briefly vibrating when struck. Available as single crashers, double, triple or quad, and ribbon crashers. The version by PJ Drums and Percussion in Denmark is called Effector.

P.J. Percussion

Crotal Bells *see* Sheep Bells

Crotales *or* Antique Cymbals

Fr. *crotales*; Ger. *Zembeln*; It. *cimbali antichi, i crotali*

usual written range - sounding two octaves higher

The origins of crotales go back thousands of years, when they consisted of two pieces of wood, bone, or bronze with a leather loop on each. They would be held on the finger and thumb of one hand and struck together—normally the dancer held a pair in each hand. In contemporary terms finger cymbals are thought of as a separate effect, and crotales are a series of bronze discs resembling tiny cymbals, but crucially, being of definite pitch. They are quite heavy, around $\frac{3}{16}$" thick, and have a diameter of around 2½"–5". They have a very distinctive high, clear bell-like sound. The most usual available range (actual pitch) is two octaves C^6–C^8, though Kolberg produces ones with a range of five octaves $G\sharp^3$–G^8 (crotales sound two octaves higher than written, similar to the glockenspiel). The first noted use of crotales in the orchestra was by Berlioz in the 'Queen Mab' scherzo from *Romeo and Juliet* with pairs of B♭ and F, and E and F in The Trojans. Debussy followed with E and B at the end of *L'Après-midi d'un faune*. It appears probable that both composers commissioned the manufacture of these crotales themselves. Stravinsky uses pairs of A♭ and B♭ for just eight bars in the first part of *Rite of Spring*, though I have never seen a printed part for this, only manuscript. Where single notes are written, the best effect is achieved by one player striking two crotales of the same pitch together, rather than striking one crotale with a beater—the two sound-waves ringing together have a better quality.

Chromatically, Messiaen uses two octaves in several works, including *Des canyons aux étoiles*, as does Henze in his Seventh Symphony. Messiaen also uses an added effect of several pitches being bowed rather than struck. This can be very effective, but the composer needs to give the player time to prepare each note—as the crotale is only resting on the stand, and not tightly fixed, it is frequently necessary to steady it at the centre with one finger to prevent the bow just sliding off the note.

Crotales, whether as single notes or as chromatic sets, now appear very frequently in contemporary writing. The larger chromatic sets now often have a damper pedal added, a great advantage: this operates in a similar fashion to the sustaining pedal on a piano. The main manufacturers are Avedis Zildjian, Kolberg, Paiste, Sabian, and Ufip.

See also Finger Cymbals

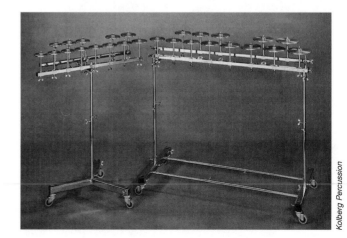

Kolberg Percussion

Cuckoo

A two-tone whistle that imitates the cuckoo.

Cuica

The cuica is a Brazilian friction drum. A thin wooden stick passes through the metal shell and one end is fastened in the centre of the single head, which has a diameter of around 5"–8". The drum is cradled in one arm while the other hand rubs the stick with a resined cloth. The head tension is changed by the fingers of the hand holding the drum, and usually has a range of around an octave. The sound is somewhat similar to the lion roar or string drum, though higher in pitch. Used in Latin American bands it is a rhythm instrument, but it is rarely used in this way in Western music. Available from PJ Drums and Percussion, Gope Percussion, and others. The fibreglass version is called a qweeka.

Cup Chimes

A set of seven miniature cymbals with large bells and narrow rims; and they have a bright, exotic sound. Available singly or in any combination; only from Paiste.

Cymbalette

Cymbalettes are several sets of tambourine jingles mounted on a cross or stick. The sound is quite similar to that of the sistrum. Used by Boulez in *Notation*. Available from PJ Drums and Percussion, and others.

See also Rocar

Cymbal Tongs *see* Metal Castanets

Cymbals

Fr. *cymbales*; Ger. *Becken* (*Tellern* for clashed cymbals); It. *piatti*, *cinelli*; Sp. *platos*

Cymbals are one of the key percussion instruments in every type of music, and everything about them, from their origins and history, through to the incredible choice of types and timbres available today, makes the cymbal a fascinating subject in its own right. The precise origins are obscure, but there is evidence of types of cymbals in ancient times, though not necessarily in the form that we know today. China and Turkey feature strongly in any history of cymbal-making, although what we in the West understand to be a Chinese cymbal today has a quite different sound quality.

The most famous name in cymbal-making is Zildjian, with an extraordinary history going back to 1623. Today the main cymbal manufacturers are Avedis Zildjian in the U.S., Sabian in Canada, and Paiste in Germany. Smaller companies include Bosphorus and Istanbul in Turkey, Meinl in Germany, and Ufip in Italy.

Cymbals are made of an alloy known as B20 bronze, a combination of 80 percent copper and 20 percent tin, with trace elements of silver. This in itself is very brittle, and the original Avedis Zildjian's discovery was a method of treating this alloy to make a casting that could then be heated and rolled repeatedly without breaking.

To say that the contemporary percussionist/drummer is spoilt for choice is a massive understatement—there are now quite literally hundreds of types of cymbal from which to choose. In the symphony orchestra the cymbal player is crucial, not least because so much that he or she plays is so very obvious to the audience. Every (honest) percussionist has known the acute embarrassment of putting a *fff* cymbal clash in the wrong place!

In the top symphony orchestras the percussion section will have an armoury of cymbals from which to choose. Again it is very much a matter of taste, but they will probably have pairs of cymbals ranging from about 13" through to the 22" or 24" likely to be used for a huge climax in a Mahler symphony, together with a wide range of suspended cymbals. Diameter, thickness, and profile determine the pitch of a cymbal: cymbals described as French are lighter and thinner with a faster sound decay, Viennese are of medium weight, and the Germanic are the heaviest. For, say, a Mahler symphony, most percussionists would opt for a fairly heavy type of crash cymbal, with a slow sound decay. (In the orchestra crash cymbals are a pair of cymbals to be clashed together—in a drumkit context a crash cymbal is a small, thin, suspended cymbal with a fairly rapid sound decay.)

Today's kit players also have a vast selection of cymbal sounds from which to choose, and it is not particularly unusual to find a star player using perhaps as many as fifteen in the one set-up.

Apart from the conventional clash cymbal effect, and the use of various types of mallet on a suspended cymbal, three other effects are worthy of note.

1. A cymbal clash of whatever dynamic is a very immediate effect—there is no "creeping in" to match a pianissimo string chord in the slow movement. One effective solution is a cymbal "slide"—sliding the edge of one cymbal across the face of the other. This is used in Puccini's *Tosca* to denote the swish of a sword on stage, and also used very tellingly in Debussy's *La Mer* and Richard Strauss's *Don Quixote*. Some conductors will suggest sliding a coin across the cymbal for a rather similar effect.
2. The use of a double-bass or cello bow across the edge of a suspended cymbal produces a wide range of harmonics.
3. For the clash cymbals the instruction "a due" means that the player scrapes or vibrates the faces of the two cymbals together. This is a difficult effect to bring off with an even sound, and some players opt to hold the two cymbals together so that they barely have contact, and employ a colleague to play a light roll with soft sticks.

Of great value to the orchestral player is the cymbal rack—an insulated or padded rack that enables the player to rest the cymbals quickly and silently. This very useful, perhaps now indispensable, piece of equipment was first introduced by the Swiss drummaker Eugen Giannini in the early 1960s, and has since been imitated by many manufacturers. Comfortable soft leather straps and pads are essential for the heavier pairs of cymbals, and the straps need to be regularly checked for wear—a cymbal flying through the air if a strap breaks can be a lethal missile. The largest crash cymbals in particular are probably better stored flat rather than on edge.

Chinese Cymbal

Fr. *cymbale chinoise*; Ger. *Chinesische Becken*; It. *plato cinese*

The Chinese cymbal has a quite different shape and sound to other cymbals. The deep central dome is squared off and the edge is upturned—the sound is short and very abrasive. It also gives a good effect with the bass bow, with a very wide range of harmonics. Chinese type cymbals are made by the main cymbal manufacturers, and the authentic instruments are available from Asian Sound, Wu Han-Chinalight, and Yuet Wah Music.

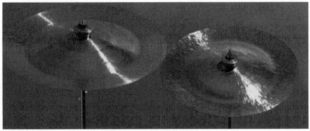

Asian Sound

Ching Ching

Ching Ching are very small pairs of cymbals from the Gamelan orchestras of the Far East. They are around 8" in diameter, have a large dome, and are made of brass. The sound is very clangy, and totally unlike the normal cymbal sound. They are used to great effect by Benjamin Britten in his ballet music *Prince of the Pagodas* and the opera *Death in Venice*. Available from Asian Sound, Wu Han-Chinalight, and Yuet Wah Music.

Hi-Hat Cymbal

Hi-hat cymbals are two matched cymbals of the same diameter fitted on to a hi-hat pedal. The bottom cymbal lies face up in a fixed position, and the depression of the pedal brings the top cymbal down until the two faces meet. The player can use the pedal alone, giving a tight sound as the cymbals meet, use snare-drum sticks on the top cymbal with the pedal closed, or open so that the cymbals vibrate together. The hi-hat is an essential part of the drumkit—most players choose cymbals of around 13" or 14". An additional optional effect is to add a ching ring or hatbourine, or the Avedis Zildjian "jungle hat"—all these use tambourine jingles to add in a rock tambourine sound.

See also Ching Ring

Sizzle Cymbal

The sizzle is a conventional cymbal with a series of rivets loosely inserted at intervals around the circumference. The effect is a continuous buzz from the rivets as the cymbal vibrates. A similar effect can be obtained by draping a light chain across the cymbal surface. A more recent innovation is to have a cluster of about three rivets, rather than having them evenly spread around the edge; this is intended to give more control, and concentrate the sizzle sound in one area of the cymbal (only available from Avedis Zildjian).

D

Dabachi *or* Japanese Temple Bell

These are in the shape of a bowl made from hammered bronze, or, for the very small ones, brass. The tone is very pure and resonant, and the diameter of the bowl may be as small as 3" or, very rarely, as large as 36". The most usual sizes found are between about 3" and 12". The larger bowls normally rest on a cushion, and are struck by a leather- or rubber-covered beater, or occasionally rubbed around the edge to produce a continuous singing tone. The very smallest are mounted on a handle and struck with a small metal beater, and these are used at the head of the procession into the temple. Temple bells appear regularly now in orchestral scores, usually as unpitched instruments, but, as the tone is so pure, specific pitches are

Asian Sound

sometimes asked for. Stockhausen uses a chromatic sequence of dabachi known as a "rin" in his work *Inori*, but the more usual use is as several different, unspecified pitches, as in Boulez's *Rituel*, George Crumb's *Ancient Voices of Children*, and Henze's *The Raft of the Medusa*. Takemitsu uses various specified pitches, each dabachi being placed on a timpani, in *From Me Flows What You Call Time*; in this instance the striking of the bell is simultaneous with the moving of the timpani pedal, giving a unique glissando effect. A wide range of temple bells is available from Asian Sound; a rin can be obtained from Kolberg.

Daiko

Daiko is the generic Japanese term for drum. Gangu daiko is a deep, barrel-shaped drum on a stand; minyo hira daiko is a shallow, double-headed drum on a stand; ryomen hira daiko is a pair of small, double-headed drums with handles, head diameter approximately 10" and depth about 4"; uchiwa daiko is a pair of small, single-headed drums with handles, similar in appearance to a large table-tennis bat. All are available from Professional Percussion, Tokyo, and Asian Sound.

Daimuru

The daimuru is hand-held and consists of two gourds back to back, with a head on each, and with two small wooden

balls hanging from a string on either side. When the drum is rotated quickly the movement throws the balls sharply against the heads, giving a dry, rattling sound, a rather similar effect to the monkey drum or klong-klong. Available from AfroTon.

See also Damaru; Monkey Drum

Daira *see* Doira

Damaru

The damaru is from Tibet, and is similar to the daimuru and the monkey drum, the one essential difference being that the two gourds are replaced by human skulls!

Darabuka

Fr. *derbouka, tambour arabe*; Ger. *arabische Trommel*; It. *tamburo arabo* (the spellings are open to many variations)

The darabuka is a goblet-shaped Arabian hand drum, with a shell of clay, wood, or metal, though the contemporary

Western versions are more likely to be of fibreglass. The size may vary quite considerably, but a head diameter of between 8" to 12" is usual; they may or may not be rod-tensioned. The genuine instrument will have a goat or sheepskin head, but the Western imitations will probably use plastic. The drum is held under one arm, and the player uses a combination of finger strokes and slaps, with damped sounds and variations of pitch by hand pressure. Darabukas are now widely available. Berlioz writes for a "tarbouka"—usually taken to be a darabuka—in *The Trojans*. Globokar includes the darabuka in both *Étude pour Folklora* 1 and 2. Available from AfroTon—Western copies are widely found.

Desk Bell

The desk bell is a small brass bell around 4" in diameter, mounted on a stand; the sound is activated by a plunger. They were frequently used in shops and offices in the first part of the twentieth century, and are more rarely seen today, but are an effect occasionally called for by composers. They can often be found in antique shops.

Devil Chaser *see* Burano

Dhol and Dholak

The dhol or dholak is an Indian double-headed, string-tensioned drum with a slightly barrel-shaped shell. Various sizes are available, but a typical dhol would be around 25" deep, with a head diameter of 13" and is played with sticks. The dholak is a smaller version, played with the hands, with measurements of around 18" depth and head diameters of 6" and 8". Available from Asian Sound and JAS Musicals.

Didgeridoo

The didgeridoo is an Australian Aboriginal instrument that occasionally finds its way into the percussion section, as in Peter Maxwell Davies's *Eight Songs for a Mad King*. It is usually formed from a hollowed-out branch of the eucalyptus tree, and may be up to around 6" in length. The player sounds the deep, fundamental note, varying the timbre with mouth and tongue in somewhat similar fashion to the Jew's harp—for the expert, circular breathing is essential! The sound can then be sustained for a considerable time, and may be varied in both pitch and volume, with rapid trillings of the tongue. The player may also produce the drone and sing through the instrument simultaneously. Didgeridoos are now quite widely available, from AfroTon and others.

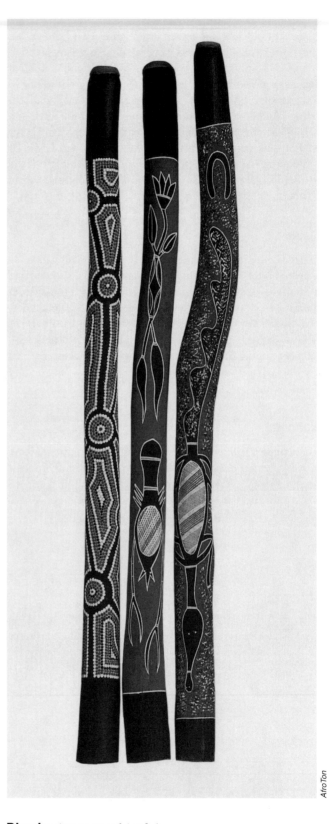

AfroTon

Djembe (pronounced *jembe*)

The djembe emanates from Africa and is a bass hand drum, goblet-shaped, usually made from mahogany with a goatskin head with rope system tensioning, though there are now many Western imitations in fibreglass with plastic heads. The player is seated, with the drum between the knees. Increasingly found in a wide variety of Western music. Available from AfroTon, Kambala Percussion, and Sabar Roots; Western versions are also widely available.

See also Kessing Kessing

Doira *or* Daira

The doira is an east European hand drum, rather like a large tambourine but with iron rings around the inside of the hoop in place of jingles. Khachaturyan included the doira in his original score of the *Gayaneh* ballet music.

Doumbek *see* Darabuka

Doumdoum

The African doumdoum has a wooden shell made from a single trunk, with cowskin heads, and is rope-tensioned. It is available in six sizes from Kambala Percussion.

Drumkit *or* Drumset

Drumkit or *drumset* is the name given to the combination of drums and cymbals for one player. The basic elements are a foot-pedal bass drum, snare drum, and hi-hat cymbals, to which are added tom-toms, cymbals, and any other instruments/effects as desired. The drumkit provides the main rhythmic thrust of a jazz or pop group. The variations are endless: a small basic kit might consist of pedal bass drum, snare drum, hi-hat pedal, two mounted tom-

Premier

toms and one floor tom-tom, and two or three cymbals. However, a star drummer might have a set with two pedal bass drums, snare drum, hi-hat pedal, eight tom-toms, fifteen cymbals, and four gongs. The cymbals will have names such as crash, light crash, heavy crash, jazz ride, classic ride, pro splash, China splash, dark Chinese, mini Chinese, and so forth. The drumkit player has total freedom of choice in his or her instruments and very wide freedom in actual playing.

The drumkit from a Premier catalogue of the 1930s was, unbelievably for us in the twenty-first century, only $72 with ivory or ebony finish, or $78 in "Wonder Finish," whatever that was! Another point of interest is that the *largest* cymbal in the catalogue was a mere 15" in diameter. Drumkits, however, have changed quite a bit since then; Korean temple blocks, Chinese tom-toms, rhythm boards, and wood blocks have long since dropped out of use.

Dulcimer

The definition of precisely what constitutes a dulcimer is, to say the least, very confusing. It is apparently mentioned in English literature as early as 1400; it is described in the 1950 *Oxford Companion to Music* as a "shallow closed box upon which are strung wires to be struck with small wooden hammers . . . hammered or plucked . . . a piano without mechanism." The *Oxford Companion* published in 1992 has a similar definition, but crucially adds that "small glockenspiels made for children have also been called dulcimers." and it is this that I have always understood to be the modern definition. Both books go on to describe the east European cimbalom as a development of the dulcimer, the strings similarly passing laterally across the player. In America there is a plucked, three-string instrument with a fretted fingerboard called an Appalachian dulcimer, also called dulcimer *tout court*. The Early Music Shop has both the Appalachian dulcimer and also the hammered instrument available. However, if it appears in today's percussion scores it is almost certainly the child's glockenspiel that is intended, as in Peter Maxwell Davies's *Eight Songs for a Mad King* and *Blind Man's Buff*.

See also Cimbalom

Dulcitone

The dulcitone was invented around the end of the nineteenth century, and is quite similar to the celeste both visually and aurally, the crucial difference being that the notes themselves are a series of tuning-forks. The sound is also similar to that of the celeste. Though apparently quite popular as a domestic instrument in the early part of the twentieth century, it has now seemingly disappeared from use. It normally had a four-octave range.

E

Effector *see* Crasher

Effects

The development of music in the twentieth century brought about a situation where any strange sound that could not be produced on conventional string, woodwind, brass, or keyboard instruments ended up in the percussion section. In effect, this brought about an extraordinary development in percussion writing that still shows no sign of abating. Some examples of the sheer scale of the composer's imagination illustrate just what the percussionist may be called upon to play—or act—or both! To take an extreme example, in Ligeti's *Adventure* and *Nouvelle adventure* the single percussionist requires

1. an open wooden box with four rubber bands stretched over it (the box to act as a resonating chamber when the rubber bands are twanged)
2. paper bags (to pop)
3. toy frog (to squeak)
4. cloth (to tear)
5. tin foil (to rustle)
6. thick book (pages to be very slowly flicked through)
7. empty suitcase (to hit)
8. tin can plus hammer
9. sandpaper blocks plus sandpaper taped to floor.
10. wrapping paper, greaseproof paper, tissue paper, and newspaper
11. cushion (to hit)
12. rack with carpet and carpet beater
13. balloon (to squeak)
14. bottle (to hit)
15. plastic cup (to crunch)
16. tray of crockery plus metal dustbin/garbage pail (crockery to be thrown into bin!)

In addition, rather more conventionally, the same player also needs xylophone, glockenspiel, bass drum, snare drum, guiro, and suspended cymbal.

Other unusual requirements include those of George Benjamin's *At First Light*, which has a ping-pong ball dropped into a glass tumbler: a suitable glass should maximize the number of times that the ball bounces. The player also has to tear newspaper (out of sight of the audience).

Richard Rodney Bennett's *Waltz from "Murder on the Orient Express"* includes a steam effect—achieved with a cylinder of CO_2. Harrison Birtwistle's *Mask of Orpheus* has a "Noh harp," a frame carrying five metal bars horizontally suspended over a timpani: the player strikes the notes and moves the timpani pedal up and down to produce an eerie sound.

John Cage's *First Construction in Metal* includes five different-pitch thundersheets, four brake drums, four gongs resting on pads, and a water gong (a gong dipped into a tub of water produces a downward glissando, and an upward one as the gong is raised). The same composer's *Third Construction* requires a North West Indian rattle, four different sets of five tin-cans, cricket callers (split bamboo), and a conch shell (to blow). In Roberto Gerhards' *Concert for Eight* the percussionist finishes the work playing with timpani sticks on the piano strings. Henze's *Voices* includes three thunder sheets, starting pistol, wineglasses, Jew's harp, three penny whistles, and a referee's whistle, and his *Don Chisciotte della Maneia* includes a few bars of mandolin in the percussion part (do I hear cries of foul from the Mandolin Players' Union?). Benedict Mason's *!* (the exclamation mark is indeed the title of the piece) requires a waterphone, binsasara, gourd in water, rainmaker, udu pot, theatre lightning, cuckoo, devil chaser, trihorn, Schwirrbogen, and patum pipes. The same composer's *Concert for the Viola Section* needs electric sirens, rainmaker, slide whistles, corrugated plastic tubes, and fishing reels.

Ligeti's original score of *Le Grand Macabre* needed twelve motor horns (three players with four horns apiece, one for each hand and foot), four music boxes, metronome, hammer, high steamship whistle, crockery plus metal dustbin, plastic cups and wood to snap in half, while his Piano Concerto has a percussionist finishing the slow movement with a Hohner harmonica in C270. Erik Satie's *Parade* includes ship's siren, two starting pistols, bouteillephone, water splash (sound of pouring water), and an old-fashioned typewriter (i.e., one with a bell at the end of the carriage slide).

Iannis Xenakis's *Persephassa* needs *galets de mer* (stones), wooden and metal simantra, and affolante (a very thin metal sheet is used). In George Crumb's *Ancient Voices of Children* Tibetan prayer stones are needed, and in addition the three percussionists have to continually shout in one number, closely followed by having to sing a triad (pianissimo) at first accompanied and then solo. In the same composer's *Songs, Drones and Refrains of Death* he writes for crystal glasses pitched in Bb^5, D^6, E, G#, and A, and a lujon (a box containing wooden resonators: over each is a metal plate, and the sound is quite distinctive, as a metallic bass marimba), Jew's harp, and three gourds. Copland's early opera *Hear Ye, Hear Ye* requires an auctioneers gavel, and Ferdé Grofe's *Grand Canyon Suite* includes a lightning machine, though I have no recollection of how we resolved that particular problem!

But the most bizarre of all composers demands (up to now) surely has to be in Mauricio Kagel's *The Compass Rose*, where the percussionist has to turn into a lumberjack and rhythmically swing an axe into a large wooden log; his other instruments include dried buddleia bushes (to wave), jugs of water, cushions, kazoos, and electric fans. I have no recollection of any preparation for this type of score from my professors at music college!

As can be seen by these few examples, virtually anything may be expected of the contemporary percussionist; even stranger, we all accept this situation as the norm.

Egg Shaker *and* **Egg Maracas** *see* Shakers

Electronic Percussion

Increasingly available as an alternative to real percussion instruments are the electronic versions, from drumkits entirely in pad form to the latest xylosynth available from Wernich. Obviously the electronic format has its uses, but it would appear that audiences (thankfully) prefer to see and hear a drummer with a real drumkit rather than the unspectacular pads. The xylosynth, which is in three-octave form, offers all the keyboard percussion instrument sounds from a single set of pads. Amazing combinations of instruments are available—the top half sounding like a marimba, the bottom half like a vibraphone, for example, and this facility will obviously be of great value in some cramped orchestra pits, but I think the real instruments will retain their attraction for both their aural and their visual appeal.

Elephant Bells

Elephant bells are small, spherical brass bells, the lower half consisting of claw-like prongs. They are occasionally called for by composers, as in Henze's *Tristan*.

F

Fan Drum *see* Daiko

Field Drum

Field drum is the American term for a deep military snare drum with a head diameter of around 14" and a depth of around 12".
    See also Snare Drum

Finger Cymbals

Finger cymbals, also sometimes called antique cymbals, are pairs of tiny brass or bronze cymbals only 2"–3" in diameter. In ancient times they were used by dancers, normally with a pair in each hand. Though usually shaped as cymbals they can also have the appearance of tiny bells. The high-pitched tinkle of the finger cymbals is by definition taken as an unpitched effect.
    See also Crotales

Fishing Reel

A fishing reel is of use to the percussionist as a really pianissimo ratchet effect, at the opposite end of the spectrum to the guttural sound of a football rattle.

Flexatone

The flexatone is a small, thin, flexible metal plate fastened to its frame at one end. The plate is hit alternatively on each side by rubber or wooden beaters mounted on a clock spring. A tremolo is the normal effect, and thumb pressure on the free end of the plate alone changes the pitch, resulting in a glissando from note to note.

Though it may seem surprising to us at the beginning of the twenty-first century, it appears that the flexatone first appeared in the 1920s as an extra effect in the early jazz bands, and was even advertised then as "making jazz jazzier." an idea that to us now seems somewhat farcical. Any possible onetime links with jazz are longpast, and the flexatone now only makes comparatively rare appearnces in the orchestral percussion section. It is usually employed as an abstract effect, since it is notoriously difficult to play specified pitches with any accuracy—the thumb pressure to sharpen or flatten is extremely subtle and difficult to gauge (to possess perfect pitch is an obvious advantage). Different sizes of flexatone obviously have differing ranges. The sound is quite clangy, a cross between the smoothness of a musical saw and a poor glockenspiel. Composers such as Schoenberg, Honegger, and Henze have utilized the unusual sound of the flexatone, but the most famous example is probably still Khachaturyan's Piano Concerto (1946) where the flexatone share the melody line with the violins in the second movement. The composer's note in the score stipulates that the flexatone should have a smooth, singing tone; otherwise it should be omitted. However, when Khachaturyan came to the London Symphony Orchestra in the early 1970s he immediately ruled out the flexatone on sight, before a note had been played, and wanted a musical saw or nothing! Just how the flexatone came to appear in the score in the first place remains a complete mystery.

Kolberg Percussion have two flexatones available, with ranges of E^5–$C\sharp^7$ and $D\sharp^4$–C^6. Steve Weiss Music (with Equilibrium), and Kolberg appear to be the only companies with the saw in their catalogues.

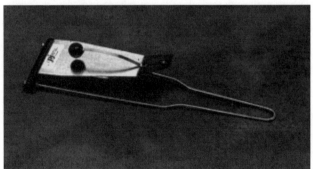

P.J. Percussion

Frame Drum

Fr. *tambour sur cadre*; Ger. *Rahmentrommel or Tamburin ohne Schellen*; It. *tamburino senza cimbali*

A frame drum is merely the name of a type of drum rather than an actual instrument. Though there seem to be differing interpretations, the most usual definition is that it is a small, single-headed hand drum with no depth to the shell, such as the Irish bodhran, or the east European doira.

Frigideira *or* Frying Pan

The frigideira is a small frying pan around 6"–7" in diameter, played with a metal rod. It is used in Brazilian carnival bands. One hand holds the pan handle, with a finger being used to damp the pan as required; the other hand obtains a variety of sounds, stopped and ringing, plus a tremolo effect from rotating the wrist. Another version has two pans on a sprung steel handle. Available from PJ Drums and Percussion and others: Kolberg also have two octaves of frying pans, from F^4 to F^6—obviously a rather different effect.

P.J. Percussion

G

Ganza *see* Chocola

Geophone

The dictionary definition of the geophone is a "device for detecting vibrations in the ground." However, as a percussion effect, most players would describe the sound as that of the ocean: some manufacturers even have a very similar instrument for schools, called an *ocean drum*. The shell is usually around 24" in diameter and 6"–8" deep; the two calf heads are tightly lapped, tacked in position, and lacquered (the instruments for schools usually have plastic heads). Inside the drum are pellets or lead shot; the player holds the instrument horizontally, and tilts it back and forth so that the pellets slide around the drumhead, giving a sound akin to that of the ocean lapping on the seashore. Messiaen used the geophone to great effect in *Des canyons aux étoiles* and *Saint François d'Assise*. These instruments are usually custom-made, though Kolberg does now offer three different sizes.

Ghana Bell

A hand-held, heavy metal double bell from Ghana, the African forerunner of the agogo bells of the samba bands.

The player uses open and stopped sounds. Available in three sizes from AfroTon, also from Kambala Percussion.

Glass Armonica (*also known as* Glass Klavier *or* Verrophone)

Fr. *armonica de ver*; Ger. *Glasharmonika*; It. *harmonica di vetro*

Invented in 1761 by Benjamin Franklin in London, the glass armonica (frequently misspelt as harmonica) once enjoyed great popularity, even tempting composers such as Mozart and Beethoven. The instrument is made up of a series of glass bowls arranged chromatically on their side, the naturals and the accidentals each on a single horizontal rotating axis; the bowls are rotated by means of a treadle or pedals, and the sound is produced by the player's moistened fingertips. All ten digits are used, enabling great technical dexterity as well as facilitating chords. However, its initial popularity waned; it seems that there are two possible reasons for this: (1) that the instrument merely went out of fashion as it were, with changing styles in music, and (2) that the instrument had an adverse effect on the player's nervous system. It now appears quite possible that the second problem was caused by players moistening their fingers from their lips rather than from a bowl of water, thus ingesting some of the lead used in the paint around the rims. This at least is a plausible explanation. (Some dictionaries state that the bowls were kept moist in a shallow trough to water: my information is that this is quite wrong, and it would in any case have altered the pitch.) Whatever really happened all that time ago can now obviously only be a matter of conjecture; what is indisputable is that there is now a great resurgence of interest in all the glass instruments.

The whole subject of the glass armonica, glasses, glass harp, and so on is worthy of detailed research. For the purposes of this book a brief synopsis follows:

1746   Gluck (1714–87) wrote a "Concert upon Twenty-six Drinking Glasses," and later said that anything that he could play on the violin or harpsichord he could also play on glasses!

1761   The glass armonica was invented by Benjamin Frankel in London.

1790   A bass glass instrument called the euphon was invented by E. F. F. Chiadni, the sound being produced by rubbing glass rods.

1865   The glass klavier was improved by Georges Bachmann, and called the *piano* harmonica: it was a five-octave instrument, the forerunner of the celeste. It was used by both Rossini and Liszt, and has now been reconstructed for the group of glass instrument musicians called the Sinfonia di Vetro in southern Germany.

The glass instruments used today are the glass armonica, the glass klavier, and the verrophone: the last of these is made of vertical glass pipes, and has a big sound with an immediate response—a surprisingly stronger sound than the glass armonica. It is very versatile, and is therefore probably better suited to orchestral use. Sascha Reckert, the leader of Sinfonia di Vetro, developed this in 1985. The glass armonica itself has no definitive range, but F^3–F^6 is adequate for most works, including the Mozart mentioned below. The sound, as one might expect, is very pure—similar in some ways to that of the organ. Very considerable technical dexterity is required to play it, but this bears only a passing similarity to piano technique.

Other composers who have written for glass instruments include Donizetti in *Lucia di Lammermoor*, Richard Strauss in *Frau ohne Schatten*, and Mozart in *The Magic Flute* and *Adagio* and *Rondo K.617* (this last for glass armonica, flute, oboe, viola, and cello—the glass armonica in part resembles a piano score, and indeed there have been many occasions when the piano has deputized, as it were, for the composer's desired instrument). The most famous example is probably still the Aquarium in Saint-Saëns's *Carnival of the Animals*: in my experience this has almost always been played on the glockenspiel, but has now been re-recorded using the specified glass armonica, at last with the sound that the composer

intended. Having now heard this, it is so very obvious why it was the composer's original choice.

Glass instruments are available from Sascha Reckert in Germany and G. Finkernbeiner in the U.S.

Glissandotrommel

This appears to be a unique production from Kolberg Percussion, being specifically designed for Stockhausen's *Momente*. The first version is a shaped drum changing pitch as the player moves up the instrument, the diameter of the head being much greater at one side and narrowing down at the other. The second is in the form of a 32" bass drum; by following a certain path around the head a glissando effect of two and a half octaves is obtained. (I have no knowledge of the technical expertise involved in achieving this effect!) The other side of the drum operates as a normal bass drum.

Kolberg Percussion

Glockenspiel (*also known as* Orchestra Bells *or* Keyed Glockenspiel)

Fr. *jeu de timbres*; Ger. *Stahlspiel*; It. *campanelli*; Sp. *timbres*

keyed glockenspiel: Fr. *glockenspiel à clavier*; Ger. *Klaviaturglockenspiel*; It. *campanelli a tastiera*

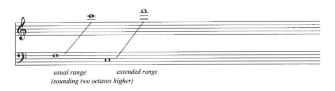

usual range   extended range
(sounding two octaves higher)

Generally known as a glockenspiel, but usually known as orchestra bells in the U.S., this is a chromatic keyboard instrument made up of steel bars—sometimes the accidentals are raised, sometimes not—the width of the bars being

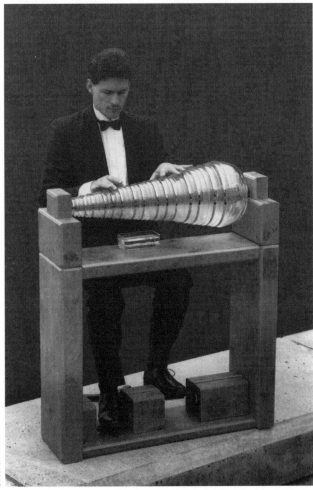

Sascha Reckert

around 1"–1½". The range is variable, two and a half octaves (F^3–C^6, written pitch) being the minimum orchestrally, but three-octave (F^3–E or F^6) instruments are increasingly popular. The glockenspiel sounds two octaves higher than written. There are also instruments that extend the range downward to C, so the *possible* overall range can be said to be three and half octaves. (Fall Creek now offers a three-and-a-third-octave version, and I know they have made a three-and-a-half-octave version to order from Graham C. Johns and the Liverpool Philharmonic.) Though glockenspiels were at one time always table-top instruments, the three-octave concert versions are increasingly provided with a sustaining pedal similar to that of the piano—a very worthwhile improvement. In contemporary terms the glockenspiel is also quite likely to be resonated. The instrument has a bright, high-pitched bell-like sound.

The usual two-and-a-half-octave glockenspiels are available from Adams, Bergerault, Fall Creek, Ludwig Musser, Premier, Studio 49, and Yamaha; three-octave instruments are available from Adams, Bergerault, Fall Creek, Lefima, Kolberg, and Studio 49. Fall Creek alone has a three-and-a-third-octave C–E.

The glockenspiel also appears as a keyboard instrument similar in appearance to the celeste. This normally has a three-octave C–C range and has an action similar to the piano, but with metal hammers instead of felt. Many composers, from Mozart in *The Magic Flute* to Debussy in *La Mer*, wrote for the keyed glockenspiel, and these parts were expected to be played by a keyboard player, *not* a percussionist. (My first principal conductor with the London Symphony Orchestra was Pierre Monteaux, who had worked closely with Debussy; he had the glockenspiel part of *La Mer* split between conventional and keyboard glockenspiel.) However, the sound quality of the keyed glockenspiel is certainly inferior, and many of these parts are now played in the percussion section on the conventional instrument, *La Mer* and Messiaen's *Turangalila* being just two examples. The huge advance in playing standards is one factor in this development; another is the much greater choice of sound quality from a percussionist with a range of mallets.

Kolberg Percussion makes a three-and-a-third-octave keyed glockenspiel, C–E.

See also Bell Lyra; Tubaphone

Gong

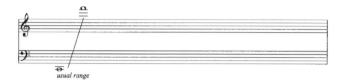

usual range

The world of gongs is without doubt one of the most complicated areas in percussion. Their history and folklore go back thousands of years, and gong-making itself is an art shrouded in history and tradition, with religion and theatre both having a significant role. The countries most associated with gongs are all in the East, in particular Burma, China, Indonesia, and Java. There are many types and weights, varying with the country of origin, but the gong is basically a circular bronze plate, usually with the rim turned over. Gongs with definite pitch will have a raised boss or nipple in the centre, which is also the striking spot. The weight is also very variable, the Indonesian type being very thick and heavy, with a very wide rim, and having a deep, sonorous, rich tone. Thai gongs are much lighter, both in weight and tone. The Gamelan orchestras of the East show off the stunning effect of the gong-chime: the Burmese version has the player sitting in the centre of a frame with the gongs mounted almost horizontally around him; in other cultures the frame may either have the gongs hanging in line or suspended horizontally in line. The series of gongs of the Gamelan orchestras are of course initially not tuned to our Western scale, but increasingly Balinese, Thai, and Javanese gongs are being exported to the West.

There is often confusion between gongs and tam-tams, but in contemporary terms players generally think of most gongs having a "straight" sound, some with an *element* of pitch, some with *definite* pitch, while a tam-tam gives a low, resonant splash of sound. However, some composers do write *gong* when they expect to hear a tam-tam, Benjamin Britten being

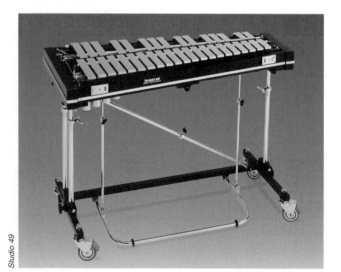

but one important example. The latest Avedis Zildjian catalogue is also confusing, with the tamtams all called gongs, and the inclusion of one 10" tam-tam gong, whatever that might be.

In today's Western music, the gongs most frequently found are Balinese or Thai; but cast gongs are made for works such as Puccini's *Turandot* by companies such as Ufip and Kolberg. A lighter type of tuned gong from Paiste is also popular, and four and a half octaves, C^2–F^6 are available. All types of Chinese gongs and tam-tams are available from yuet Wah Music. Balinese gongs are available from PJ Drum and Percussion, and Thai gongs from Asian Sound, Kolberg, and Steve Weiss. The main cymbal manufacturers also have a variety of gongs in their catalogues, some of which are imported from China but then have the cymbal company's logo added.

Lighter-type gongs that are hammered into a specific pitch may likewise be found to be knocked out of pitch by continual heavy playing or use of unsuitable mallets. The heavy cast gongs are obviously virtually free from this possibility.

See also Chinese Opera Gong; Tam-Tams; Thai Gong; Water Gong

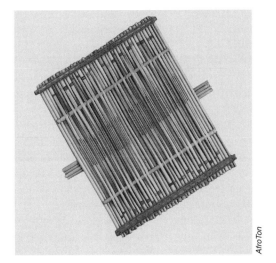
AfroTon

Gong Drum

The term frequently used for a single-headed bass drum, mostly popular in Britain.
See also Bass Drum

Goumbe

The goumbe is a large hand drum, the African equivalent of the conga. It is carved from a section of tree trunk, has a cowskin head, and is rope-tensioned. Available from Afro-Ton in five sizes.

Gourd in Water *see* Waterdrum

Grass Harp

The grass harp is from Cameroon, and consists of plaited strings of savannah grass tensioned in a frame. When stroked, it gives the gentle sound of the wind on grass. Available from AfroTon.

Guiro

A Latin American rhythm instrument, originally a gourd with a serrated surface. The sound is produced by rubbing a small wooden stick across the serrations or notches, and the player varies the sound with the position and pressure of the scraper. Now produced in a very wide variety of shapes and sizes, using both wood or fibreglass, the frequency and depth of the serrations are obviously the crucial factors in determining the sound quality. Available universally.
See also Reco Reco

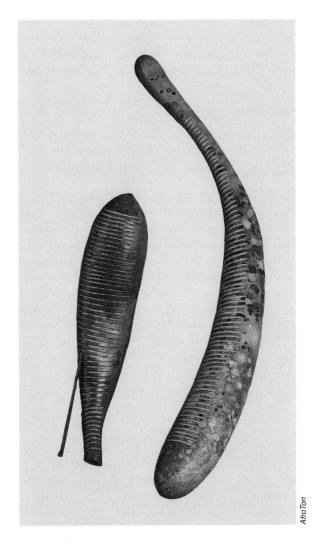
AfroTon

Guiro Woodblock

A PJ Drums and Percussion effect of incorporating a serrated edge along the top of a woodblock, thus giving the option of a guiro effect together with the woodblock.

H

Hammer

Fr. *marteau*; Ger. *Hammer*; It. *martello*

As the name implies, this is quite literally a hammer blow, and can create a great dramatic effect, as used by Mahler in his Sixth Symphony and Berg in his *Three Pieces for Orchestra*. A very large wooden tent mallet is usually employed, but the player has to use his or her own judgement about the best thing to hit. According to the hall, this may be the stage itself or a small rostrum. In most concert halls today the stage has a basic concrete construction with a facing of wood: where this is the case it may even be found that lifting one end of a small rostrum and banging the rostrum itself down will produce the necessary resonance. The hammer blow can be very effective—the player should keep an open mind and be prepared to adapt to the acoustics of the hall.

The Kolberg catalogue includes a hammer effect, in this instance a large, resonating wooden box, with hammer.

Handbells

Handbells are probably the oldest form of bell known, but for music in the twenty-first century we have handbells of different sizes which obviously have pitch but are thought of as unpitched, and we have several octaves of handbells made specifically for the popular pastime of bellringing. Orchestrally, handbells have been employed by a number of composers: if more than four or five are needed they are probably mounted and set out as a keyboard, usually for a single percussionist to play with mallets. Examples of orchestral use include Percy Grainger with four octaves plus in *The Warriors*, Peter Maxwell Davies with a D♭ major scale in *Worldes Blis*, Henze with three octaves in *Voices* and nine different pitches in *Requiem*, and Benedict Mason with three octaves in *Concerto for the Viola Section*. The Whitechapel Bell Foundry offer six and a

half octaves, G^1–C^8 (the bottom G weighting 18½ lbs), and Kolberg three octaves.

Hatbourine

A line of mounted tambourine jingles designed to fit on top of a hi-hat pedal to add a rhythm tambourine effect—a similar effect to a ching ring. Universal Percussion in Ohio has both these effects, plus a jingle head: a snare-drum head with four sets of tambourine jingles built in to the head. Avedis Zildjian also have a "jungle hat"—six sets of tambourine jingles built in to a hi-hat cymbal.

Hi-Hat Cymbals *see* Cymbals

Horses' Hooves

The sound of horses' hooves is an effect going back to the days of the silent films and music hall. The most common way of reproducing a realistic sound is to use the two halves of a coconut shell drummed on the floor.

Hourglass Drum *see* Talking Drum

Hyoshigi (*also known as* Concussion Blocks, Kabuki Blocks, *and* Kabuki Clappers)

A Japanese effect, hyoshigi are two blocks of hardwood around 7" long, each with one surface slightly convex. The two curved sides are struck sharply together to produce a high-pitched, very penetrating sound. Available from Kolberg and Professional Percussion.

I

Ice Bells

Ice bells are shaped as an enlarged cymbal dome, with a diameter of between 7" and 10", producing a hard, penetrating, sustained "icy" sound with few overtones. They are frequently used in pairs for high and low accents. Available from LP, Ufip, and Sabian.

Indian Bells

Small brass bells with clappers.

J

Japanese Temple Bell *see* Dabachi

Japanese Woodblock *see* Mokubio

Kolberg Percussion

Jawbone (*also known as* quijada)

Fr. *quyada*; Ger. *Schlagrassel*; It. *mascella d'asino;* Sp. *guyada*

A Latin American instrument which seems now to have fallen out of use to a large degree, being superseded by the vibraslap. The jawbone is literally the lower jawbone of an ass with the teeth wired loosely in their sockets and some tiny bells added. The side of the jawbone is slapped with an open hand, or scraped with a beater, so that the teeth briefly vibrate in their sockets. As the two sides of the jawbone are joined only at the front, the strain is quite considerable and it is not unusual to find a jawbone that snaps into two at the first slap! It was presumably this unreliability that led to the invention of the vibraslap by LP. The original jawbone is now difficult to locate—vibraslaps are available universally.

See also Vibraslap

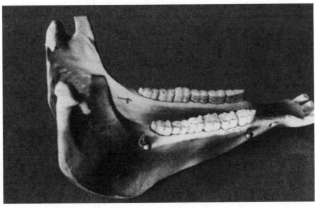

Ian Dickson

Jew's Harp *or* Jaw's Harp

Fr. *guimbarde*; Ger. *Maultrommel*; It. *sciacciapensieri*; Sp. *trompa*

The Jew's harp, or jaw's harp, is known in various forms in many parts of the world, and dates back at least to Anglo-Saxon times. Even the origins of the name itself appear very obscure, though it was apparently known in England in the Middle Ages as Jew's trump. Its one-time popularity is very difficult for us today to comprehend, especially when the *Oxford Dictionary of Music* tells us that, even as recently as 1935, there was a company in Birmingham, England making 100,000 *a week*, and that a single order from the U.S. was for 160,000!

It is obviously not a percussion instrument as such, but of course it does appear in percussion scores from time to time. The instrument consists of a very small frame of steel rod, oval-shaped, with an opening from which two sides then form a funnel. Fastened at the bottom of the rounded base and then appearing through the end of the funnel is a steel blade bent into a prong at the end. The oval part of the frame is held by one hand against the parted teeth, the blade being twanged by the other hand. The fundamental note is in the bass register, the player then moving tongue and cheeks to keep changing both pitch and volume. (Some have specific fundamental notes, some are made at random.) With practice a certain amount of control over the pitch is possible; sometimes just a steady drone is required.

In Austria the Jew's harp was at one time apparently used for serenading, and the Tyrol region was famous for the playing of two instruments at the same time, tuned basically to the tonic and dominant; today instruments with two blades are available for this. (Apparently there was a nineteenth-century virtuoso named Eulenstein who joined *sixteen* together with sealing wax, one of his party pieces being variations on a Rossini aria!) Fortunately for the Western orchestral percussionist, only very basic skills are normally required. George Crumb writes for a large Jew's harp in *Songs, Drones and Refrains of Death*, as does Lucas Foss in *Thirteen Ways of Looking at a Blackbird*. Jew's harps are quite readily available, but for those looking for a more specialized choice and information, Zoltan Szilagyi in Hungary would seem to be the person to contact. Reading his catalogue listing *eleven* different models confirms the realization that there is rather more to this instrument than appears at first sight to a layman like myself!

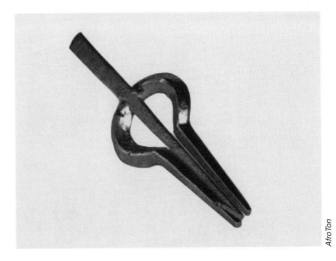

AfroTon

Jingle Head

An effect from Universal Percussion incorporating four sets of tambourine jingles into a snare-drum head, adding a rhythm tambourine sound to that of the snare drum.

Jingling Johnny *see* Turkish Crescent

Jungle Hat

An effect from Avedis Zildjian: six sets of tambourine jingles are built into a hi-hat cymbal.

K

Kabuki Clappers *or* **Kabuki Blocks** *see* Hyoshigi

Kalengo *see* Talking Drum

Kalimba or Kalimbaphone (*also known as* Sansa, Marimbul, Mbira, *and* Thumb Piano)

There are many names and varieties of this mainly African instrument. It has a wooden box resonator with sound-board on which a number of narrow, usually metal, tongues are clamped. The length of the tongues is adjustable and thus determines the pitch. The number of notes varies, but is usually between nine and seventeen, the player using his or her thumbs to activate the tongues.

Marimbula is another name for the kalimba, but is also used for the Western chromatic instrument marketed by Kolberg and others as a two-octave (C^3–C^5) instrument, and it is this version that Henze has used in *El Cimarrón* and his Violin Concerto No. 2.

The sound, whether of an ethnic or Western version, is of course not powerful, and may well need amplification if used in the orchestra. Kalimbas are available from AfroTon and Sabar Roots Percussion in Germany, World Beat percussion in the U.S., and others.

AfroTon

Kayamba

The Kayamba consists of woven reeds tensioned on a small wooden frame—giving a similar effect to the grass harp.

Kazoo

The kazoo is a wooden or metal tube with a membrane. The player hums into the tube to obtain a "buzz" from the membrane.

Kessing Kessing

This is the snare effect for the djembe, and consists of a thin metal plate with iron rings attached at the edges, which can be tied to the rope tensioning of the drum. Available from AfroTon and Sabar Rotos Percussion.

Kettledrums *see* Timpani

Key Chimes

An abstract effect somewhat similar to the pin chimes, made up of a large number of metal keys suspended from a wooden bar. Available from AfroTon.

AfroTon

Keyed Glockenspiel *see* Glockenspiel

Klong-Klong *see* Monkey Drum

Kokiriko *see* Binsasara

Kring

The kring is a hollowed-out section of tree trunk with several slits in the top: the player uses wooden sticks to play on the various surfaces, which of course provide a variety of pitches. The kring is used for religious music in Guinea, Mali, and Senegal. Available from AfroTon and Kambala Percussion.
See also Log Drum

Kyisi *see* Burma Bell

L

Lambeg Drum

The lambeg is a double-headed, rope-tensioned bass drum for the Irish marching-bands. It has a much larger depth of shell than a normal marching-band bass drum, usually being wider than the player, and both heads are normally struck with a cane.

Lion Roar (*also known as* String Drum)

Fr. *tambour à cordes*; Ger. *Brummtopf*; It. *ruggio di leone*; Sp. *tambour con cuerdes*

The lion roar is a friction or string drum, and is found in various forms in both Africa and South America. The instrument known in Western music is a smallish, single-headed drum with a gut string or cord passed through the centre of the head and fastened. The taut string is resined and the player slides a piece of leather or cloth up the string to produce a sound similar to the roar of a lion. Probably the most famous use of the lion roar is by Varèse in *Ionisation*, *Hyperprism*, and *Amériques*.

Usually the player needs both hands for this effect, one to hold the string taut, and the other to slide the cloth: Kolberg has the drum mounted, with the string held, and the player then needs only one hand to turn the handle to activate the roar.

Kolberg Percussion

Lithophone (*also* Stones)

Fr. *pierres*; Ger. *Kieselstein*; It. *sassi*

The lithophone—the word comes from the Greek *lithos*—stone is a chromatic mallet percussion instrument with notes of marble or stone. In various forms the musical properties of stone have been utilized since ancient times. Much more commonly, the sound of two small stones being struck together is also an occasional percussion effect. The pitch is dictated by the size and type of stone and the amount of pressure applied if both stones are gripped—the highest sound will be obtained if one stone lies flat on the palm of the hand and is struck by the other. Another effect is for one stone to be placed on a timpani head and rubbed with the other—the natural resonance of the drum will enhance the sound, George Crumb writes for Tibetan prayer stones in *Ancient Voices of Children*, but I know of no Western percussionist who has managed to provide the genuine article.

However, it would appear that our understanding and musical knowledge of stones today is as nothing compared to our forebears of the eighteenth and nineteenth centuries. Apparently a Peter Crosthwaite of Skiddaw in the Lake District in England was the first person to discover the musical properties of Skiddaw slate. His journal for 11 June 1785 reads: "This morning found six musical stones at the end of Long Tongue on the sand beds of the river Creta." The intonation of these six notes was perfect, but the remaining ten of his set took a further six months to find, and many hours a day to tune. This was done by carefully chipping away at the stone until the desired note was achieved. He then used this set of sixteen notes to attract visitors to the museum that he had founded in Keswick in 1780. Later, a Joseph Richardson, who came from a family of stonemasons but was apparently also regarded as something of a musical genius, collected various rocks with a pure tone from the same area, and then took thirteen years to shape enough individual notes to make up a *seven*-octave range. In 1840 he and his three sons started to undertake concert tours with great success, the repertoire including selections from Handel, Mozart, and Beethoven, and arrangements of waltzes, quadrilles, galops, and polkas. Apparently, considerable variations in tone were achieved by using different methods of striking the notes, which created a blend of organ, piano, harp, and flute sounds, though we are told that "the full power of the instrument often had to be withheld for fear of the safety of the window glass!" In the late 1840's they updated the lithophone by adding octaves of steel bars, Swiss bells, drums, etc., and even played at Buckingham Palace at the command of Queen Victoria. This was so successful that two further concerts were requested. The band also toured in France, Germany, and Italy, which in the middle of the nineteenth century must have been a major achievement in itself. A concert tour of the United States was planned, but had to be cancelled just before departure date because of the sudden death of one of the players.

Later sets of musical stones include the "Till Family Rock Band" (a slightly different understanding of the term *rock band* I think!), which did tour the United States in the late 1800s. This instrument is now in the Museum of Orange, New Jersey.

Today the lithophone appears very rarely, and I have never been asked for one in all my playing career. Kolberg

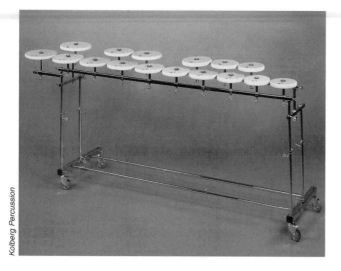

Kolberg Percussion

has a two-octave version E6–E8, but the notes appear to be cast circular discs, and so I would imagine that the tone quality is somewhat different from the nineteenth-century instruments mentioned above.

Log Drum *or* Slit Drum

Fr. *tambour de bois*; Ger. *Schlitztrommel*; It. *tamburo di legno*

Traditionally a hollowed-out wooden log, around 2'–3' long, used as a signalling drum and found in different forms in various parts of the world, usually with just two tones. In

contemporary usage there are many types available, with up to ten different pitches per drum. It is normally, of course, of indefinite pitch, but Kolberg has a chromatic octave available, C^3–C^4. It is also available from AfroTon (called *kring*), and a wide variety of Western versions are available from Schlagwerk Klangobjekte.

See also Kring

Lujon *or* Loo-Jon

The Lujon is a type of metallophone developed in the U.S., with a thin metal plate of sprung steel screwed down at one side and projected over a wooden box resonator. It has a distinctive tone, perhaps best described as a metallic bass marimba sound. It is played with soft mallets, and of course has limited volume. The original lujons had only six notes, but larger ones are now available. Berio uses the lujon in *Circles*, as does Henze in *Scenes and Arias from the 'Return of Ulysses'*. The Kolberg catalogue has a lujon, F^2–F^3.

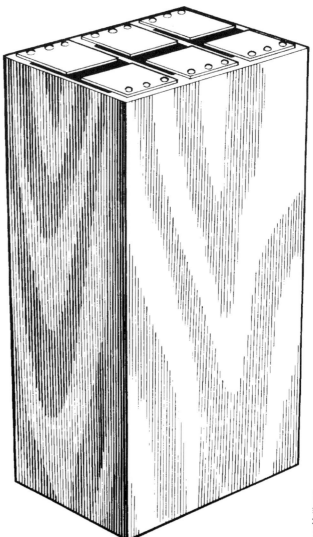

Tony Matthews

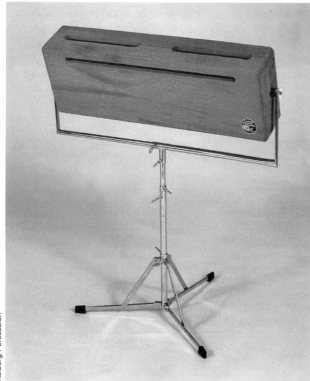

Kolberg Percussion

M

Maracas

Maracas are gourd rattles from the Latin American bands. Used in pairs, the gourds have a handle attached and contain some seeds or pellets. Today, of course, a variety of materials is used, in place of both the gourd and the seeds. For the orchestra, the composer may specify a light or heavy sound, and may also indicate a high or low pitch.

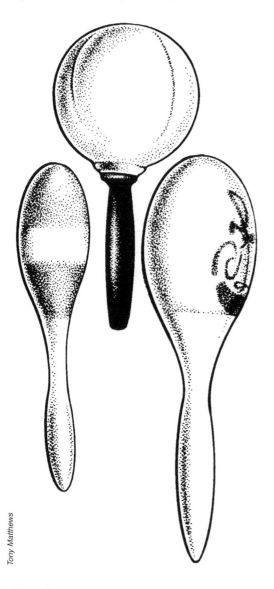

Tony Matthews

Marching Men

This is another effect required by the drummer in the days of the silent films, this time to re-create the sounds of an army on the march. It consists of a wooden frame loosely holding some thirty or forty wooden dowels about 1" by 5"; the player moves the frame up and down so that the dowels strike the floor to produce the required effect of marching feet. Available from Kolberg.

Marimba

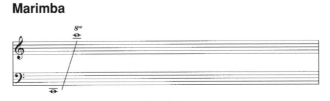

In appearance the marimba is the big brother of the xylophone, having wooden bars and metal resonators, but there the similarity finishes. The normal tone of the xylophone is very hard and dry; the marimba's qualities are much softer and warmer.

The bars of the marimba are wider and thinner than those of the xylophone, and softer mallets are used. The instrument known in Western musical culture today was developed in the U.S. in the early part of the twentieth century, appearing in small ensembles and vaudeville, and a large boost to its popularity came with a concert at Carnegie Hall in 1935 by the virtuoso Clair Omar Musser with a 100-piece marimba band. However, the marimba's history comes from Latin America, Mexico in particular. Marimba bands are still an important part of Mexican culture, and include huge six-and-a-half-octave instruments played by several players together. The *nabimba*, or *nadimba*, was a marimba with small pieces of vellum placed across the top of the resonators, adding a buzzing quality when the bar was struck—quite popular apparently in the early part of the twentieth century, but it now appears to be extinct (merely writing this is probably a virtual guarantee that there will be a nadimba revival!). Percy Grainger scored for both marimba and nadimba in his suite *In a Nutshell* written around 1914.

In Western music, the last quarter of the twentieth century saw the development of new playing techniques, much-improved instruments with a greater range, and a vastly enlarged repertoire; this has all helped to revolutionize both the marimba and marimba playing. The professional models available today range from four octaves, the standard four and a third, A^2–C^7, known as a *concert grand*, a four and two-thirds, E^2–C^7, and the now accepted soloist five-octave C^2–C^7 instrument, which encompasses all the solo marimba repertoire (there is now even a world marimba competition). Bergerault also has a five- and a third-octave marimba. In the past it was the four and third-octave concert grand that was used most frequently in the orchestra, but several manufacturers now have extensions available so that the bottom range can be added as and when required. The bars of the marimba are usually of rosewood: as with the xylophone, the use of composite materials may be suitable for student models, but these are not generally adequate for professional use.

Playing techniques that have now been developed, by Gary Burton (jazz vibraphone virtuoso) and Leigh Howard Stevens in particular, have revolutionized writing for the marimba, and artists of the calibre of Keiko Abe, Robert Van Sice, and Leigh Howard Stevens are now soloists of international renown.

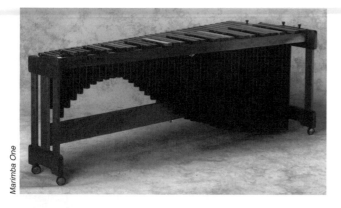

Marimba One

The main manufacturers of marimbas are Adams (Holland), Bergerault (France), Ludwig Musser (U.S.), Malletch (U.S.), Marimba One (U.S.), Studio 49 Royal Percussion (Germany), and Yamaha (Japan).

Marimbula *see* Kalimba

Mark Tree

The mark tree is a set of approximately forty small brass tubes, graduated in length from around 4" to 12" and suspended in line from small to large. The player strokes a beater or finger across the tubes to produce a shimmering upward or downward glissando effect. Now widely used in all types of music, the graduated line of tubes in order of length is the most usual version, but all sorts of variations on this are also now available. The largest choice is from Asian Sound.

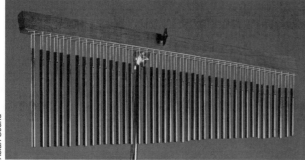

Asian Sound

Mbira *see* Kalimba

Metal Castanets *or* Cymbal Tongs

Fr. *castagnettes de fer*; Ger. *Metallkastagnetten*; It. *castagnette di ferro*

As one might expect from the name, metal castanets are two finger cymbals around 2" in diameter. The player has a pair in each hand and plays them as one would play castanets.

The shells may resemble those of wooden castanets, but the sound is obviously quite distinct, and this is a very rarely used effect, although Saint-Saëns does employ both normal and metal castanets in his opera *Samson and Delilah*. A rather different version, often referred to as cymbal tongs, has the two metal cups mounted on a sprung steel hoop—these are usually played by striking on the knee. Available from Avedis Zildjian, Kolberg, and others.

Metallophone

The metallophone as such is rarely called for today. The instrument existed in the ancient Gamelan orchestras of the East, being similar in appearance to a trough xylophone but with bronze bars instead of wood. The nearest instrument in modern usage is a vibraphone without motor and with open resonators. A metallophone was the instrument that Britten had in mind when writing *Prince of the Pagodas* and *Death in Venice*. Sonor and Yamaha appear to be the only companies with any type of metallophone currently in their catalogue.

See also Lujon; Vibraphone

Metronome

The constant clik-clak of the conventional metronome was used to great effect by Ravel at the start of his opera *L'Heure espagnole*. He asks for three metronomes set at speeds of 40, 100, and 232—a small problem being that most metronomes now have a top rate of 208. Ligeti employs a metronome in his opera *Le Grand Macabre* (there is also the extraordinary Ligeti novelty *Poème symphonique* written for 100 metronomes).

Mexican Bean

A dried bean pod usually around 12"–14" in length. When the pod is shaken the seeds inside produce a very dry, staccato rattle. Berio uses this effect in *Circles*. Sometimes difficult to locate, but now available from AfroTon.

AfroTon

Microxyl

The microxyl is an instrument invented and built by English percussionist and composer James Wood for his percussion quartet *Village Burial with Fire*, and also used in his *Two Men Meet, Each Presuming the Other to be from a Distant Planet*. One player has four microxyls, each consisting of thirty-six pieces of ramin dowel of 1¼" diameter; these are laid horizontally over a resonating box and are all tuned to a specific number of centimeters apart. A fifth microxyl is used by another player: this is elliptical and has forty-seven pieces of dowel. The dowels are stroked, rather than struck, by wooden xylophone mallets.

James Wood

Military Side Drum

Fr. *tambour militaire*; Ger. *Militartrommel*; It. *tamburo militar*; Sp. *tambor militar*

The term for a deep snare drum.

Mini Timbales *see* Timbalitos

Mokubio (*also known as* Japanese Woodblock)

The mokubio is a circular block of hardwood resting on three small feet, with a conical resonating chamber carved out from the underside. The sound is high-pitched and very

Kolberg Percussion

penetrating—rather higher and sharper than the conventional woodblock. Boulez uses mokubio in *Rituel: In memoriam Bruno Maderna*. The diameter is usually 4"–12". Normally of indefinite pitch, but Kolberg has a one-and-a-half-octave range available.

Monkey Drum (*also known as* Klong-Klong)

A small double-headed drum with a handle attached; two small balls or beaters are attached to a string on either side. When the drum is rotated quickly the movement throws the balls alternatively against the heads, giving a dry, rattling sound. Found in various forms in Africa and Asia, variously used to scare monkeys, or by beggars. A similar effect is the diamuru which uses gourds to form the drum, and in Tibet there is the damaru—apparently made from two inverted human skulls! Available from AfroTon and Kolberg.

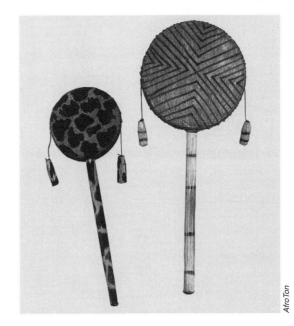

AfroTon

Motor Horns *see* Car Horns

Musical Saw

Fr. *scie musicale*; Ger. *Säge*; It. *sega*

This is a blade of fine steel similar to a carpentry saw but minus the teeth. It is normally played with a bass bow, the blade being held and bent into an *S* shape by one hand and bowed with the other, the pressures of the holding hand dictating the pitch. It has a resonant singing tone and is without the clanging of the flexatone. A vibrato is obtained by slightly shaking the end. The musical saw was once very popular in music halls and vaudeville, but is now rarely seen. As with the flexatone, the pitch can only be changed by a slide from one note to another, and to play with any degree of accuracy is extremely difficult. However, there are of course experts in this, and it can be *very* effective in the right circumstances. It was certainly used to great effect by

George Crumb in *Ancient Voices of Children*, and it would appear that it was the musical saw, rather than the flexatone, that is prescribed in both score and parts, that Khachaturyan wanted for the slow movement of his piano concerto. Tishchenko's Third Symphony requires a saw for both percussionists. Equilibrium (marketed by Steve Weiss) and Kolberg appear to be the only companies making the musical saw.

N

Nabimba *or* **Nadimba** (*also known as* Buzz Marimba) *see* Marimba

Nakers

Nakers appeared in England in the Middle Ages and were probably brought back from the Crusades. The precursors of todays timpani, they usually have copper or clay bowls and were used in pairs hung around the player's waist and played with leather or wooden beaters. Nakers are available from the Early Music Shop and Lefima.

Noh Harp

An effect devised by Harrison Birtwistle for his Mask of Orpheus. Five metal bars are suspended on a horizontal frame over a timpani, and the player strikes the bars and simultaneously moves the timpani pedal up and down. The resulting sound waves are a unique mix of metallophone and timpani. Made by Arthur Soothill to the composer's specification.

O

Octobans (*also known as* Rockets)

Octobans closely resemble boobams both visually and aurally, but are made in sets of eight and are presumed to be unpitched, though yet again there obviously is an element of pitch.

Ogororo

These are small discs with diameters of 5"–9". The sound is high-pitched and silvery. Available from Ufip.

Orchestra Bells *see* Glockenspiel

Pandeiro *or* Pandero

The pandeiro is a Brazilian samba band instrument, closely resembling the tambourine, though with rather fewer sets of jingles, producing a drier sound; a head diameter of between 10" and 14" is usual. The player uses one finger to dampen the head and the other hand in a combination of slaps, finger strokes, and heel of the hand and thumb rolls.

In the samba bands the pandeiro is also thrown in the air and acrobatically spun around the body. Available from PJ Drums and Percussion, and others.

Piano Pins *see* Pin Chimes

Piccolo Snare Drum

The piccolo snare drum is the highest-pitched snare, usually with a shell depth of no more than 3" and probably having a smaller head diameter of around 13". Also sometimes known as a soprano or sopranino snare drum.

Pin Chimes (*also known as* Piano Pins)

Pin chimes consist of around forty small metal pins suspended in lines on several cords—they produce an abstract type of sound that is somewhat similar to that of the mark tree. Available from Asian Sound, PJ Drums and percussion, and others.

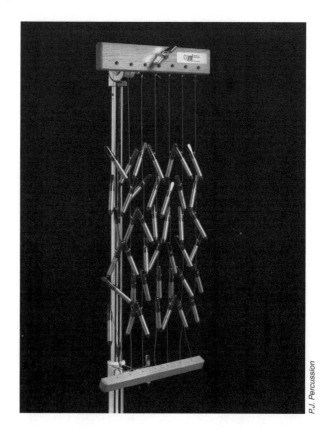

Pistol

The pistol shot is an occasional effect in the orchestra: Satie's *Parade* was probably the first example, Copland's early opera *Hear Ye, Hear Ye* and Henze's *Voices* being just two other examples. A starting pistol with blank cartridges is normally used.

The Satie work requires the pistol to follow a very simple rhythm; to avoid the embarrassment of the gun "jamming," it is safer to use two pistols. I once tried vainly to assure an elderly conductor that the player *could* read the written rhythm, but if the trigger is pulled twice in very quick succession, the second attempt does not always produce the desired result!

Pop Gun

The pop gun is used to imitate the popping of a champagne cork. The effect has been used by many composers from Johann Strauss onwards. Available from Kolberg and PJ Drums and Percussion.

P.J. Percussion

Pot Drum *see* Udu Pot

Q

Quattro Bell

Four square bells similar to cowbells, built as a graduated set, giving the player a wide variety of bell sounds. Available from PJ Drums and Percussion.

P.J. Percussion

Quijada *see* Jawbone

Qweeka *see* Cuica

R

Rainmaker *or* Rainstick

Rainmakers were originally thick sticks of bamboo or cactus with loose seeds inside: when the stick stood on end the seeds very slowly trickled down, giving a fair imitation of the sound of rain. The sticks may be anything up to around 6' in length, and the "rain" then lasts a considerable time—the sound is of course limited in volume. Now available in different forms and sizes, including fibreglass copies and a circular tube from Meinl, where the player turns a handle and the rain can last forever! Rainmakers now appear quite regularly in contemporary scores. The genuine article is available from AfroTon and World Beat Percussion. Western imitations are widely available.

Ratchet

Fr. *crecelle*; Ger. *Ratsche*; It. *raganella*; Sp. *carraca, matraca*

The origins of the ratchet are obscure, though at one time they were used in Roman Catholic churches during Holy

Kolberg Percussion

P.J. Percussion

Week. Today the ratchet comes in various forms and is an effect used by many composers. A cogwheel depresses thin wooden tongues that are clamped in the frame at the opposite end; as the cog turns, the tongues individually click over the spokes. The heavier ratchets have a large cog and produce a heavy, guttural crackel—it is these types that were once used by football fans, the weight of the ratchet swinging it around the handle.

Those usually used by the orchestral percussionist have a crank attached to the handle, so that it is the cog itself that turns, the frame remaining stationary. This way the player has much more control, and is able to produce an even, continuous sound.

The weight of the ratchet used obviously varies according to the effect desired; a heavy, "football-type" sound is needed for Strauss's *Till Eulenspiegel* while a much quieter and more refined sound is necessary for Ravel's *L'Heure espagnole*. For a really *pianissimo* effect, a reel from a fishing rod can be an excellent substitute.

Both Kolberg and PJ Drums and percussion have several sizes and weights available, Kolberg additionally offering the heavier versions with a resonating box.

Rattle Board

The rattle board gives a sound similar to playing on a table with metal sticks. Available from PJ Drums and Percussion.

Reco Reco

The reco reco is a Brazilian bamboo scraper similar to the guiro but having a sharper, more abrasive sound. There is also now a spring reco reco (see photo): one, two, or three springs stretched across a resonating chamber and scraped with a metal beater. Reco reco are widely available, spring reco reco from Kolberg or PJ Drums and Percussion.

See also Guiro

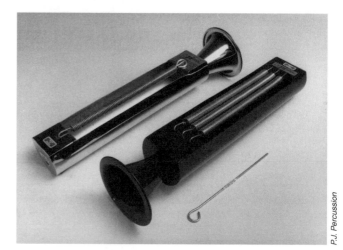

P.J. Percussion

Repenique *or* Repique

Repenique is a small Brazilian metal-shelled drum, usually from about 8" diameter and 10" depth to 12" diameter and 12" depth. It is played with one hand and one snare-drum stick, using a combination of stopped and ringing sounds, buzz rolls, and rimshots. Available from PJ Drums and Percussion, and others.

Ride Cymbal

The ride cymbal is the name given to cymbals used in a drumset situation where a continuous rhythm, rather than single beats, is required.

Rin *see* Dabachi

Rocar

The rocar is made up of twenty to thirty sets of tambourine jingles mounted on a stick or metal frame, and is used in the samba bands. They are very similar to cymbalettes.

P.J. Percussion

Rockets *see* Octobans

Rotosound

Rotosound is a bronze disc between 7" and 9" in diameter, introduced by Paiste. The surface tapers off towards the edge, and a special holder allows the disc to rotate, giving a vibrato effect with a very slow sound decay.

Rototoms

Invented in the early 1960s by American percussionist and composer Michael Colgrass, the rototom is a tunable tom-tom with no shell—in effect a tunable drumhead. A lightweight alloy frame connects the counterhoop to a central spindle: turning the drum clockwise raises the pitch; anti-clockwise flattens it—there is usually a range of approaching an octave on each drum. The realistic *overall* range is about three octaves for the best sound quality, and rototoms are now a very useful addition to the percussion armoury. These drums are sometimes used chromatically

P.J. Percussion

and sometimes unpitched. A glissando of sorts is possible by turning the drum with one hand while playing with the other, but a pedal-operated rototom is also available. They are made in seven sizes from 6" to 18" diameter and are now widely available. Tippett writes for two octaves, C^3–C^5, in *Byzantium*, and three octaves, E^2–F^5, in *Rose Lake*.

The space needed for two or three octaves can be a crucial factor: if the piece is written for one player it *may* be possible to mount the drums one octave behind another; if for more than one player, as in both *Rose Lake* and *Byzantium*, virtually the whole range has to be mounted as a single keyboard, and the 20' to 30' of stage width required for the rototoms alone can be problematical.

Rute *or* Switch

Fr. *verge*; Ger. *Rute*; It. *verga*

The rute is a bunch of twigs or a bamboo stick split at one end into a number of tongues. Mozart and Haydn both employed this effect, the rute playing the accompanying beats and a normal drumstick played the accented beats. The switch was used either on the bass drum head or the shell of the drum. Subsequently Mahler used this effect in several symphonies, though in a somewhat different style. The rute was the forerunner of the wire brushes that were introduced originally for jazz drummers. The split bamboo type of rute is found in some Asian and Polynesian countries.

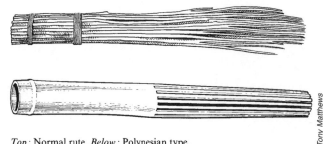

Top: Normal rute. *Below:* Polynesian type.

Tony Matthews

S

Sabar

A hand-carved waisted drum from West Africa made from a single wooden trunk with a goatskin head. It may be used as a hand drum or played with a stick. Originally used for village ceremonies and social occasions. Available from Afro-Ton, Sabar Roots Percussion, and others.

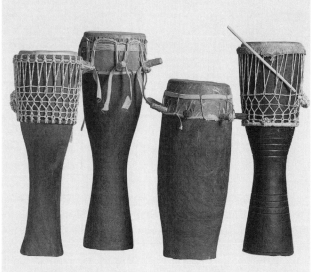

AfroTon

Samba Whistle *see* Apito

Sanctus Bells

Fr. *clochettes pour la messe*; Ger. *Messklingeln*; It. *campanelle da messa*

Sanctus bells are used in the ritual of the Roman Catholic Church before Holy Communion and the Benediction, and consist of four small brass bells of different pitch attached to a small frame with a handle. They occasionally appear in orchestral works, John Tavener's *The Whale* and *In Alium*, and Martinů's *Military Mass* being but three examples. Most Roman Catholic cathedrals also have a shop close by selling religious artifacts and books, and this is also the place to find sanctus bells—additionally, Kolberg stocks them.

Sandpaper Blocks

Fr. *papier de verre*; Ger. *Sandblöcke*; It. *ceppi di carta vetro*; Sp. *papel de lija*

Sandpaper blocks were once an essential part of a drummer's kit in the days of music hall and silent films, but today they appear rather less frequently. Since the sound can vary considerably, composers should always specify the grade of sandpaper, fine, medium, or rough. John Adams uses sandpaper blocks in "The Chairman Dances," and rough sandpaper (not blocks) in *Nixon in China*. Ligeti uses sandpaper in *Adventure*, both in the conventional way and also taped to the floor for the player's feet!

Sansa *see* Kalimba

Saw *see* Musical Saw

Schellentrommel *see* Tambourine

Schlitztrommel *see* Log Drum

Schwirrbogen

The schwirrbogen is a bow mounted on a stick with a handle, with elastic stretched across the bow. When whirled

Bell Percussion

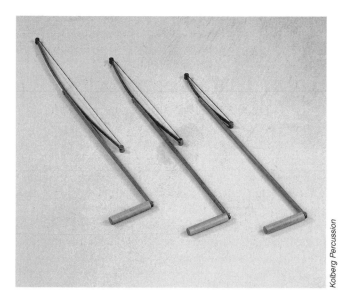

Kolberg Percussion

around the player's head the elastic gives a whining sound, which changes pitch according to the intensity of movement. Available from AfroTon, Kolberg, and others.

Shakers

Shakers is a general term used in contemporary percussion terminology to cover virtually any hand-held rhythm instrument containing dried seeds, grain, or similar—thus egg shakers, etc.; spinner eggs are similar to egg shakers, but the sound is produced by spinning the top of the egg. Produced by PJ Drums and Percussion.

Sheep Bells (*also known as* Crotal Bells)

Sheep bells are the tiny bells once hung around the necks of grazing sheep, and are virtually identical to individual sleigh bells. In Britain, at least, they are still frequently unearthed by metal detectors.

Shekere

The shekere was originally a large gourd or calabash with loose bead netting strung around it. It originated in West Africa and found its way to Latin America in the days of the slave trade. The player can rhythmically strike the beads against the gourd, slide them across the surface, or hit the bottom with the palm of the hand for a bass sound. In some ways the shekere is similar to the smaller cabaca, and now appears in all types of Western music. Today the modern fibreglass imitation seems to be most widely used. The soloist uses a shekere to great effect in Joseph Schwantener's *Concerto for Percussion and Orchestra*. Both ethnic and Western imitations are now very widely available.

AfroTon

Sheng

A set of five silver-bronze discs with a rough surface, from 9" to 13" in diameter; the sound is similar to the Chinese bells of the Ming period. Available from Ufip.

Side Drum *see* Snare Drum

Simantra

A solid piece of hardwood about 2" × 4" and usually 4' or 5' long. It was traditionally struck with a wooden mallet by Greek Orthodox Monks, each side producing a different pitch. Used by Xenakis in *Psappha* and *Persephassa* and by the English percussionist and composer James Wood in *Rogosanti*.

Siren

Fr. *sirène*; Ger. *Sirene*; It. *sirena*; Sp. *sirena*

The siren is another instance where the one name is used for several effects.

1. The mouth siren, as used by music-hall and silent cinema drummers: this produces a high wailing sound, the pitch varying with the intensity of the blowing. When the blowing ceases, the volume and pitch quickly subside.
2. The hand-cranked siren produces much the same sound but with more power, is obviously more controllable, and can be sustained ad lib. Crucially, however, it cannot be readily stopped—the sound can only die away gradually.
3. The electric siren gives much more power and control. As used in Varèse's *Ionisation* and *Amériques* an automatic cut-out is essential, so that the pitch and volume can be built up and then stopped dead at the silent bars. Both the electric siren and the hand-cranked siren can

A Ship's foghorn. **B** Electric siren. **C** Manual siren. **D** Mouth siren. **E** Klaxon.

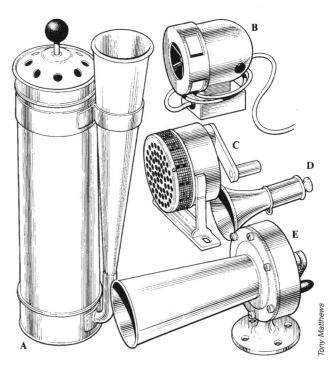

Tony Matthews

be found in different pitches—Varèse's *Ionisation* calls for both low and high sirens.

4. The ship's siren or foghorn is a very different effect, having a very low, rough, gravelly sound at a fairly level pitch.

Sirens, of whatever type, have been required by many composers. Satie's *Parade* requires siren and ship's siren, Shostakovich's Second Symphony has a siren pitched in F♯, in this case as a straight note. Hindemith's *Kammermusik No. 1* includes a siren in the final few bars: presumably a mouth siren was used when the work was written, but the electric version is rather more effective.

All the different types of siren are available from Kolberg.

Sistrum

Fr. *sistre*; Ger *Sistre*; It. *sistro*

The sistrum is one of the oldest known percussion instruments, being used in religious rites in ancient Egypt. It is usually a bronze strip bent into a loop with a handle, with some metal rods loosely fastened across the loop. The rods frequently have a number of metal rings or jingles added. Spurs are somewhat similar in sound, the jingles being added to a straight rod.

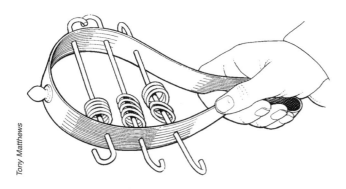

Tony Matthews

Sixxen

Invented by Xenakis for his work *Pleiades* which was written for Les Percussions de Strasbourg. "Sixxen" derives from six (the number of players in the group) and "xen," the first three letters of the composer's name.

There are nineteen keys made of aluminum section (like a square gutter upside-down). They are not tuned chromatically, even though recent designs have them laid out as a keyboard. The interval between each bar may be between a semitone and a tone. In *Pleiades* there are six sixxens; in each one corresponding bars are tuned slightly out from each other, creating a microtonal haze when they are played in unison. Though used by several European percussion groups, it appears impossible to find a current manufacturer.

Sizzle Cymbal *see* Cymbal

Slapstick *see* Whip

Sleighbells

Fr. *grelots*; Ger. *Schellen*; It. *sonagli*; Sp. *sonajas*

Sleighbells are small, spherical bells with a narrow slit and a steel ball or pellet inside. They are usually found as an unpitched effect with a number of the bells on a leather strap or mounted on a stick. Since the Middle Ages sleighbells have been used on the harnesses of horses and other animals; in the orchestra they are most usually employed as an abstract effect. Mahler uses sleighbells to supplement the woodwind quavers at the start of his Fourth Symphony, but in fact Mozart was the first composer of note to use them, with sleighbells pitched in C, E, F, G, and A in his German Dances. As a pitched effect several bells with the same note are attached to each strap—a range of two octaves, C–C, is the most usual. Available from Kolberg.

P.J. Percussion

Slide Whistle (*also known as* Swannee Whistle)

Fr. *sifflet à coulisse*; Ger. *Lotosflöte*; It. *flauto a culisse*

The slide whistle is a narrow tube usually about 1" in diameter and between 6" and 12" long. It has a mouthpiece at one end and a movable wire rod inserted at the other which moves a diaphragm up and down the tube, shortening or lengthening the column of air and thus changing the pitch. It is very simple to play if only an abstract glissando effect is required, but, as with the flexatone, very difficult if actual pitches are required. Obviously different sizes of whistle will provide differing ranges of pitch. Many composers have utilized the slide whistle: Ravel's *L'Enfant et les sortilèges* and George Crumb's *Music for a Summer Evening* are just two examples. The Crumb work (written for two pianos and two percussionists) is extraordinarily difficult to bring off accurately: the percussionists have independent liens to play, but crucially these are in unison with the two pianos. Both Kolberg and PJ Drums and Percussion have a variety of sizes available.

Slit Drum *see* Log Drum

Snake Rattle

Two long, sprung-metal tongues with a small metal pod on the end of each, with metal rivets inside to simulate the sound of a hissing snake. Available from PJ Drums and Percussion.

Snare Drum *or* Side Drum

Fr. *caisse claire*; Ger. *Kleine Trommel*; It. *tamburo piccolo*; Sp. *caja clara*

The snare drum is another of the key percussion instruments and is found in all types of music, having evolved over several centuries from different types of drum and tabor, the snare itself originally consisting of just one or two strands stretched tightly across either head. Today the snares are against the lower head, and will probably consist of twelve to twenty strands of wire, nylon, gut, silk, and wire, etc.; and these give the drum its very distinctive sound. Military snare drums are more likely to have gut snares, jazz or pop versions tend to have wire, and in an orchestra all types are likely to be encountered. The drum has a lever at the side, the snare release, which lifts the snares away from the drum head—the drum will then sound like a fairly high pitched tom-tom. When they are used in an orchestra the player should always try to have the snares off when not actually playing, so that they do not vibrate when activated by other instruments, especially the horn section.

Particularly in Britain the snare drum has been known as the side drum, because in military bands it was traditionally placed and played on the side of the left leg. This necessitated gripping the sticks with the left hand, which was held with the palm up, the stick passing under the thumb and resting on the middle finger, and the first and second fingers resting on top; the right hand was held palm down with the stick being gripped between thumb and forefinger. This is termed the "traditional grip." Today a large number of players opt for the "matched grip," where both hands grip the sticks in the same way, similar to the right hand of the "traditional grip." The snare drum is played with sticks of hardwood tapering at the playing end to a small "acorn." The type and weight of stick is very much a matter of taste, also governed of course by the type of music, and, in classical music, even the particular work being played. To take an extreme example, much lighter sticks will be needed for the second movement of Bartók's *Sonata for Two Pianos and Percussion* than for, say, a Shostakovich symphony.

The standard orchestral instrument has a diameter of 14" and a depth of 6", but of course there are many variations—the shell is usually metal, but is sometimes made of wood. The piccolo snare drum—the highest pitched—will have a shell of depth of probably only 3", and may have a slightly smaller head diameter of 13". The military snare drum the lowest pitched will have a deeper shell of around 12"–15", and a head diameter of 14"–15". Playing the snare drum re-

quires mastery of one of the core percussion techniques, the roll being made up basically of double beats with each stick as opposed to the single-stroke timpani roll. Apart from the drum, with or without snares, another effect is the rimshot, where the stick strikes the head and the rim simultaneously, *or* one stick is held down firmly across the head and rim and struck with the other stick: the resultant sound is akin to that of a gunshot. In a jazz or pop context the player also makes great use of the effect of holding one end of the stick on the drumhead with the other end striking the rim, producing a sound halfway to a full-blown rimshot. The use of wire brushes instead of sticks is also another effect widely used.

There can much confusion over the names of snare drums when used in the orchestra, in particular between the snare drum and the piccolo snare, and the terminology is now so confusing that it is almost impossible to be dogmatic about any particular composer's intentions.

Soprano *or* Sopranino Snare Drums *see* Piccolo Snare Drum

Sound Discs

Sound discs, produced by Paiste, are small, flat bronze discs giving a high, bell-like, bright sound. Though somewhat similar to crotales, the sound discs do not have definite pitch, and are best played strung up, one above the other. The five sizes range from 4¼" to 5¾".

Sound Plates

Sound plates are bronze plates similar in appearance to bell plates, but again are not of definite pitch. They produce a wide range of harmonics and have a very long sustain. The four sizes range from 7½" × 10½" to 12½" × 17¾".

Spanish Cencerros

Spanish cencerros are cowbells with a tube-like shape, ranging from about 2" to 15" in length. Available from Asian Sound and others.

Spinner Eggs *see* Shakers

Spoons

Two spoons, usually metal, but sometimes made of wood (see photo). They are held with one hand, the first finger between the handles of the spoons, and struck on the knee and by the other hand. These were widely found in the music hall, and used by street buskers and at domestic celebrations; it is yet another effect that the percussionist may be called on to provide! PJ Percussion has a pair of wooden spoons on a sprung handle—with two of these the player can play the rhythms directly on the knee.

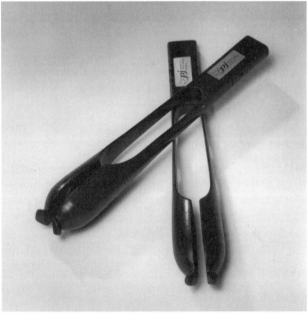

P.J. Percussion

Spring Coils

Another effect borrowed from the automobile, the coils are the springs used in car and truck suspension. When they are suspended and struck with a metal beater the sound is akin

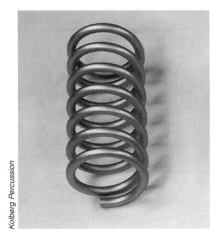

Kolberg Percussion

to that of a very unrefined triangle, i.e., with many overtones. The effect has been employed by a number of composers, Berio in particular, in Folk Songs, Laborintus II, and Epifanie. Again, Kolberg is the only source—apart from breakers' yards!

Spring Reco Reco *see* Reco Reco

Spurs

The jingle of a horseman's spurs are an occasional effect found in operetta, Johann Strauss's *Die Fledermaus* being one example. The sound is somewhat similar to that of the sistrum—usually achieved with a few metal discs strung loosely on a rod.

Squeeze Drum *see* Talking Drum

Steel Drum *or* Steel Pan

Fr. *tambour d'acier*; Ger. *Stahltommel*, *Calypsotrommel*; It. *tamburo d'acciaio*

The steel drum as a musical instrument dates from the Trinidad carnival bands of the 1930s, and from its original very basic beginnings has now been developed to such a degree that some of the world's most esteemed composers have been impressed and included steel drums in their works. The popularity of steel bands has now spread to many parts of the world, especially where there is a significant West Indian community. In Britain they are tremendously popular in schools, where extraordinarily high performance standards are achieved and at the same time many children are introduced to the great enjoyment of music making and of being a part of the band.

To make them, large steel oildrums are cut down, leaving one end with part of the shell of the drum as a resonator. The top is grooved to make a number of bubbles or domes in the surface—these form the notes, and the player uses small light sticks of bamboo or similar, around 8" long. The ends are bound with elastic bands or rubber. Because of the extraordinary evolution of steel drums (their history is a fascinating subject on its own), there is an absolute myriad of names, types, and ranges of drum, and it would appear to the layman that some standardization is now urgently needed. A typical range might consist of:

bass set	6 drums
cello set	4 drums
baritone set	3 drums
guitar set	2 drums
tenor set	2 drums
alto set	2 drums
soprano or lead	1 drum

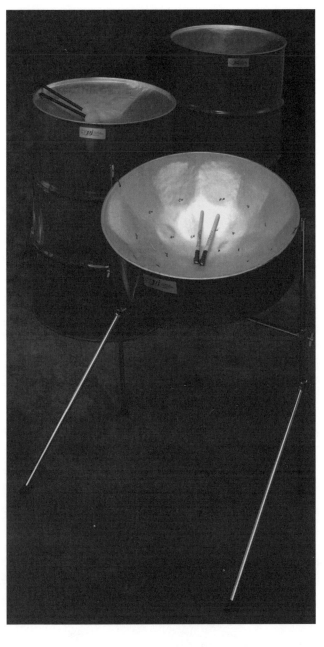

P.J. Percussion

Available from AfroTon, Asian Sound, Kolberg, PJ Drums and Percussion, Sabar Roots Percussion, Tony Charles, and Steve Weiss Music.

Note: The steel drum mallets are very lightweight, but using vibraphone or other mallets as an alternative in order to produce greater volume is not an option—it only results in knocking the instrument out of tune. Some conductors and composers need to be educated in this!

Stones *see* Lithophone

String Drum *see* Lion Roar

Sun Bell

The sun bell is a series of about ten or twelve cone-shaped cowbells fanning out from a metal hoop. Another effect available from PJ Drums and percussion and others.

P.J. Percussion

The overall range could be said to lie between about G¹ and F⁶. The highest-pitched pans, with around thirty notes, are likely to be set out in the pattern of the outer notes around the pan clockwise in fourths, with the higher octave on a corresponding inner circle, and the highest notes in the centre. The quality instruments made today are chromium plated, which apparently enhances the tone quality and also helps to ensure the durability of the intonation. Boulez wrote for alto steel drums in *Visage Nuptial*, and Henze the lead pan in *Voices*, *King of Harlem*, and *Appassionatamente*, and alto and lead in *Tristan*. Bernstein, in his Mass, and Haubenstock-Ramati, in his opera *Amerika*, have also written for steel drums. Judith Weir's *Storm* requires two alto pans to be played conventionally, *plus* three unpitched oil drums to be hit.

Surdo Drum

The surdo is a large, double-headed, usually metal-shelled drum from the Brazilian samba bands, available in a variety of sizes, usually about 14"–24" head diameter, and with a depth of about 24". It is played with one stick, the wooden beater being covered with leather, and the free hand is used to muffle as required. Available from PJ Drums and Percussion and others.

Swannee Whistle *see* Slide Whistle

Switch *see* Rute

Swordstick

The swordstick is another occasional effect, jingles being attached to either side of a blade shaped like a sword, the sound being close to that of the sistrum.

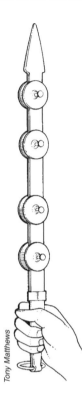

Tony Matthews

Synthesiser *see* Electronic Percussion

T

Tabla

The tabla is a pair of small Indian hand drums: the bhaya, or banya, on the player's left, and the tabla, or daya, on the right. The bhaya is the lower-pitched drum, has a metal shell with a head diameter of around 9", and slightly resembles a naker or small kettledrum. It has two layers of skin and a small, circular black patch about 3" in diameter, which is slightly off-centre. The tabla has a wooden shell, narrower at the top, a head diameter of about 6", and a height of about 12"—both drums sit on cushioned rings. The head diameter of the tabla is made up of three layers of skin and has a similar black patch about 3" in diameter in the centre. The patches appear to be of rubber, but are a composite of flour and black ashes. The head of the tabla is laced with leather thongs, and the player precisely sets the head tension by means of small wooden dowels. The playing technique uses the

Kolberg Percussion

palm, fingers, and fingertips, and, for the bhaya only, the heel of the hand is also used to press near the rim and slide towards the centre to produce a small upward glissando. The technique is extremely intricate and requires a very long apprenticeship. Very few Western percussionists have mastered the tabla, and therefore they rarely appear in orchestral music apart from single, repeated notes, as in Boulez's *Rituel: In memoriam Bruno Maderna*, which uses their unique timbre. (Berio includes a tabla in his *Circles*, but this is an error, his desired instrument being a talking drum.) Interestingly, Ravi Shankar's Sitar Concerto has a bongo player front-of-stage with the sitar soloist, the bongos being required to take the place of the tablas. (For the first performance—by the London Symphony Orchestra conducted by André Previn around 1970—the bongo soloist Terry Emery had to have several sessions with Ravi Shankar to learn how to produce tabla-type sounds!) Available from JAS Musicals Ltd. and others.

Tabor *or* Tambourin

Fr. *tambour provençal*; Ger. *provenzalische Trommel*; It. *tamburo provenzale*

The tabor was a very popular drum in the Middle Ages, but the precise definition today seems to be elusive: the most usual concept is a deep-shelled drum with a small head diameter which normally has a single gut snare across the top, or batter head, but there is certainly a variety of beliefs and expectations which have to be accepted. There is also confusion because the spelling of tambour*in* is so close to tambourine. In the German language tambourin is a tambourine; in French tambourin signifies the long drum without snares. The instrument required for the Farandole in Bizet's *L'Arlésienne* is definitely the long drum without snares, and *not* a tambourine—conductors please note! Tabors are available from the Early Music Shop.

Talking Drum (*also known as* Squeeze Drum *or* Hourglass Drum)

The talking drum is shaped like an hourglass and appears in slightly different guises and names in various parts of the world: the Nigerian version is the kalengo, in Ghana and Senegal it is the tama or dondo, and in Japan the tsuzumi. The drum is narrower in the centre and the two heads are braced together by cord or leather; it is held under one arm and played with a hook-shaped beater or the hand. The player changes the pitch by squeezing the waisted part of the drum, this making the drum "talk"—this is a unique signalling and communicating instrument. Available from AfroTon, Professional Percussion, Kambala Percussion, and Sabar Roots Percussion; there are also, of course, many Western imitations.

AfroTon

Tama *see* Talking Drum

Tamborim

A small, single-headed hand drum with a diameter of around 6" from the Brazilian samba bands. The sound is high-pitched and penetrating. The player has a stick in one hand and uses the holding hand to muffle and stop the sound as required. Available from AfroTon, PJ Drums and Percussion, and others.

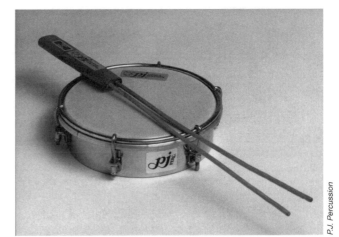

P.J. Percussion

Tambourin *see* Tabor

Tambourine

Fr. *tambour de basque*; Ger. *Schellentrommel, Tambourin*; It. *tamburo basco*; Sp. *pandereta*

The tambourine is one of the oldest known percussion instruments, and is found in varying forms in many parts of the world. The head diameter is usually between 6" and 12" and the shell, which may be of wood or metal, has a depth of about 2½". The shell has a series of horizontal slots cut out in it, each with two metal discs loosely inserted on a metal pin. A small tambourine may have a single row of six or seven pairs of jingles; a larger one will have two rows with a total of around sixteen to twenty pairs. The head is normally of calfskin and is nailed to the shell so that the head is tightly tensioned. There are tambourines with plastic heads, but the preference in the orchestra is usually for calf. The plastic-headed version may also be rod-tensioned, which of course makes it a little heavier and more cumbersome.

The tambourine is shaken and struck with the free hand or fingers or on the knee. For short, dry sounds the instrument needs to be kept horizontal so that the jingles vibrate for the shortest possible time. Thus, for a trill with a sharp cut-off, the player shakes the tambourine vertically, finishing by simultaneously hitting the head and turning the instrument to a horizontal position. A *pianissimo* trill is obtained with a moistened thumb or finger which slides from the bottom upwards around the edge—this effect is of course limited in duration as the thumb dries out or reaches that point on the circumference where a change of direction becomes inevitable! However, Kolberg now have a brilliant addition to the percussionist's armoury with a tambourine that can be held by a central spindle, facilitating not only extended thumb trills, but also enabling a change in the head tension, and also giving the player much more control and choice of sound. The central spindle may also be slipped onto a special stand, and the player can then rotate the tambourine with one hand

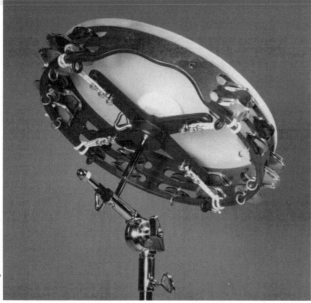

Kolberg Percussion

while producing a thumb roll of unlimited duration with the other hand. Another important Kolberg innovation is the facility to change the type of jingles on the tambourine very easily, giving the player an amazing choice of timbre. Other occasional tambourine effects have included flicking the jingles with the fingers (Walton's *Façade*), and even at the end of Stravinsky's *Petrushka*, dropping the instrument on the floor—for this the tambourine has to be held around 12" off the floor and dropped so that the whole rim hits squarely. It may also be mounted on a stand and played with sticks, as in Stravinsky's *Soldier's Tale*. The tambourine used in a rock or pop idiom is a tambourine without a head, normally shaken from side to side in a rhythmic division of the main beat. Apart from the unique Kolberg instrument, all other types of tambourine are available universally.

See also Hatbourine; Timbrel

Tam-Tam (1)

The tam-tam is expected by most players today to be of indefinite pitch, being a low, very resonant splash of sound. It is basically a flat bronze disc, which may or may not be turned over at the edge. Different makers obviously produce tam-tams with different characteristics—the thicker the metal, the longer the instrument takes to speak. It would appear that Paiste tam-tams are probably the most popular in professional use today: they have a very comprehensive range available, from about 20" diameter, through to a massive 80". Most symphony orchestras will now have a range from which to choose, with a 38" or 40" diameter being the instrument for most of the general repertoire: the very large tam-tams of between 40" and 80" are generally only suitable as an occasional effect. Though different timbres can be achieved by varying

the beater and the beating spot, a fairly large diameter is needed to ensure a very low, resonant, fundamental tone.

Naturally, the beaters for a large tam-tam need to be of a certain weight in order to bring out the full tone of the instrument. They will normally have a core of hard rubber or felt, covered with lamb's wool or similar. Padded hammers are also useful, especially where the player needs the tam-tam to "speak" immediately. Other effects include the scraping of a metal beater over the surface, or around the edge. (The bumpy surface of the edge of the Paiste tam-tam lends itself to this, and is ideal for the scrape required in Stravinsky's *Rite of Spring*.) Hitting the instrument with a metal beater must always be done with great discretion if a fatal crack is to be avoided—fortissimo is definitely not recommended. Other occasional effects called for are the scrape of a plastic soap dish across the surface and the use of wire brushes or a double-bass bow—this last produces very effective harmonics. There is also "superball"—an ordinary, high-bouncing child's rubber ball on the end of a stick, which is dragged across the surface of the tam-tam to produce all sorts of groans and squeaks.

Obviously, the tam-tam is an instrument of indefinite pitch, but different sizes in ascending or descending order may be called for to produce a graduated range of pitches, as in Boulez's *Rituel: In memoriam Bruno Maderna* and several Messiaen works.

Available from Asian Sound, Avedis Zildjian, Paiste, Savian, Ufip, and others.

See also Gong

Paiste

Tam-Tam (2)

Tam-tam is also, very confusingly, the name of an East African hourglass-shaped drum with a single goatskin head and traditional peg tuning. Fortunately for Western percussionists, it appears only rarely. Available from AfroTon.

AfroTon

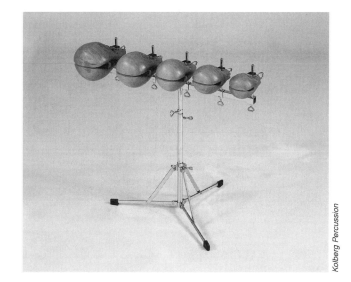

Kolberg Percussion

Tapan *or* Tupan

The tapan is a double-headed, rope-tensioned drum from the Balkans, similar to a small bass drum or large tenor drum. It is played bass-drum style with a stick, leather-covered mallet, or a switch. Globokar writes for the tapan in *Étude pour Folklora* 1 and 2.

Tarol (*also known as* Caixa)

The tarol is a Brazilian piccolo snare drum, around 12" in diameter and with a depth of about 3"–4½"; it has a metal shell and coiled wire snares. It is used in the samba bands and is played with snare-drum sticks for accents and buzz rolls. Available from PJ Drums and Percussion, and others.

Temple Blocks

The temple block comes from the East, particularly China, Japan, and Korea: in China it is called a muyu, in Japan a mokugyo, and in Korea a moktak. It is normally carved from camphor wood, is hollowed out in the centre, and has a horizontal slit, thus somewhat resembling the mouth of a fish. It is in fact sometimes known as the "wooden fish," and some temple blocks are ornately carved, the stem perhaps being shaped like a fish tail; frequently the the craftsman's initials are engraved on the side. In some countries the temple block is part of everyday religious ritual, hence the name. The size varies enormously, from the smallest, around 2½" across and hand-held, to the largest of around 30" across, which sit on a cushion in the temple—in this instance the sound is more akin to that of a muffled tom-tom.

In the West, temple blocks of up to around 9" or 10" diameter were used in the music halls and by the early jazz drummers. Today they appear frequently in the orchestra, sometimes singly, but more often in a run of several blocks. The tone is somewhat less sharp, and is darker and rounder than the conventional woodblock.

Temple blocks are normally taken to be unpitched, though Adams and Kolberg both now also have chromatic sets available. Henze's *Requiem* requires one and half octaves, C^4–G♯. The Western-made temple blocks are sometimes of wood, but increasingly of unbreakable synthetic material, with an inevitable slight difference in tone quality.

Traditional temple blocks are available from Asian Sound, Professional Percussion, and Yuet Wah Music; Western imitations are widely available.

Tenor Drum

Fr. *cassa roulante, tambourin*; Ger. *Rührtommel*; It. *cassa rullante*; Sp. *caja rodante*

A tenor drum is a cylindrical drum with a head diameter of about 16" or 18", and a depth of at least 12"—the shell may be of wood or metal. In the orchestra the head is usually of calf-skin, but it may be of plastic. In Britain and the U.S. the tenor drum is taken to be unsnared, but in other parts of the world may be expected to be snared or unsnared. It is available universally.

Thai Gong

Thai gongs are quite readily available in the West, the usual range being four octaves, C^2–C^6. Although the tone quality is good, it must be remembered that these gongs are fairly light in weight, and instruments that can be hammered into

Asian Sound

a certain pitch can similarly be knocked out of tune—this, of course, is not a problem with the heavier type of gong or the cast gongs.

See also Gong

Thai Plate Bell *see* Burma Bell

Theatre Lightning

Theatre lightning is a thin, flexible metal strip about 24" long and 5" wide, suspended from a conventional cymbal stand. When struck, it produces a very short, high-pitched splash of sound. Available from PJ Drums and Percussion.

P.J. Percussion

Thumb Piano *see* Kalimba

Thundersheet

Fr. *machine à tonnerre*; Ger. *Donnerblech*; It. *lastra del tuono*; Sp. *lamina metalica*

The thundersheet is a suspended thin metal sheet, which crackles when shaken to produce a fair imitation of thunder. Various sizes may be asked for: Henze requires three of different pitch for his *Voices*. More usually a single large thundersheet of around 4' × 8' is required, as for Richard Strauss's *Alpine Symphony*. This has always been an effect obtained by percussionists from outside sources, but Sabian now have two small thundersheets in their catalogue: 18" × 26", or 20" × 30".

Thunderstick *see* Bull Roarer

Tibetan Prayer Stones *see* Lithophone

Timbales

Timbales* are the middle-range drums of Latin American music. The two shallow, single-headed drums, with head diameters of about 13" and 14", or 14" and 15", have metal shells and are suspended either side of a centre rod. For Latin American music the heads are tightly tensioned, and the drums are played with light wooden sticks, without taper or acorn. A variety of sounds and timbres is obtained by striking the head, the rim, and the outside of the shell. In this context, cowbell(s) will probably be added to the set-up. When used in the orchestra, timbales are more frequently employed for a tom-tom sound, perhaps in conjunction with bongos, to make a run of four fairly high pitches. Available universally.

See also Timbalitos

*Very confusingly, the word *timbales* in French means "timpani."

P.J. Percussion

Timbalitos *and* Mini-timbales

Timbalitos are smaller timbales, with head diameters of around 8" and 10", or 10" and 12"—these are quite widely available. Mini-timbales, marketed by LP and PJ Drums and Percussion, have head diameters of only 6" and 8". Obviously all these have a higher basic pitch than normal timbales.

Timbrel

Timbrel was the name given to the tambourines of the Middle Ages. Available from the Early Music Shop.

Timpani (*also known as* Kettledrums)

Fr. *timbales*; Ger. *Pauken*; It. *timpani*

Timpani, or kettledrums (a term now rarely used), can be traced back to about the thirteenth century in European, and, like several other instruments, appear to have been brought back to western Europe from the Crusades. Their original form was as nakers, which were hung around the player's waist and struck with leather or wooden beaters. These developed later into use with military bands, sometimes mounted in a carriage, or more frequently slung either side of a horse, as still seen today in Britain with the mounted bands of the Household Cavalry. In the sixteenth and seventeenth centuries the kettledrummer was a person of considerable status: distinguished percussionist and historian James Blades tells us that in Germany in 1623 an Imperial Decree established The Imperial Guild of Trumpeters and Kettledrummers, the members being entitled to considerable privileges. The seventeenth century also saw the first use of timpani in the orchestra—the bowls were usually of copper, and the head diameters could vary widely, from a pair of 19" and 22", to a pair of about 24" and 27". A series of tuning handles around the hoop stretched the head over the bowl and the drums were usually tuned in fourths, and were treated as transposing instruments, being scored in C in the bass clef with the actual pitches indicated above the stave. Even at this early stage there can be confusion over composers' intentions. The roll is normally indicated by the abbreviation *tr*. Sometimes continuous groups of semiquavers or demi-semiquavers (sixteenth or thirty-second notes) were written, and, depending on tempo, these bring the effect up to what amounts to a roll. If the final pause bar of a work has the timpani written out in demi-semiquavers, the poor player has the problem of how to cope with the conductor's long pause; a normal timpani roll is the usual remedy, unless of course the conductor has other ideas! A landmark work appeared in 1685 with the *March for Two Kettledrummers* by the Philidor brothers—the instruments were tuned to G and C for one player, and the E and G abvoe for the other. a century later saw the *Concerto for Eight Timpani and Orchestra* by Johann Carl Fischer.

Among other composers of the eighteenth and nineteenth centuries who developed the use of timpani in the orchestra, the names of Beethoven and Berlioz are of special note. Berlioz brought a whole new approach to percussion in general, and timpani in particular: he appears to have been the first composer to specify the type of timpani stick to be used, and expressed surprise and disgust that other composers should have omitted such directions. The reduced timpani part of his famous *Grand messe des morts* requires a mere ten players and sixteen drums (the original score required twenty players with thirty-two drums!). The nineteenth century also saw developments to shorten the time taken to retune the timpani. The first idea was a single master key which brought the straining counterhoop up or down with equal pressure. By the 1850s there was a system to rotate the whole drum—clockwise to raise the pitch, anticlockwise to flatten it. The 1880s saw the first pedal-operated drum, the German Dresden model, which incorporated a ratchet system for the pedal, with the refinement of a master key and the first tuning gauge: the player could pre-set the gauge and then be able roughly to retune by eye. The early twentieth century saw the introduction of the balanced pedal action from Ludwig in the U.S., and a different style of ratchet pedal from Premier in Britain.

Berlioz, of course, had had a great influence on the development of orchestral composition as a whole: his use of timpani in the orchestra was revolutionary, and all the great composers who followed developed quite naturally on the foundations that he had laid. A brief comparison of the timpani writing of Tchaikovsky and Mahler, on to Stravinsky and Bartók, with that in, say, a Haydn symphony, shows how the demands on the orchestral timpanist have increased. The pair of drums of the Baroque period had developed to sets of three and four. Nielsen was probably the first to write *glissandi* for the timpani. In his Fourth Symphony, *The Inextinguishable*, written around 1915, he calls for two timpanists placed one on either side of the orchestra, with glissandi in minor thirds between the two players. Bartók extended the timpani still further with moving bass lines. However, the hand-tuned drums had a slow death in the symphony orchestra, and as recently as the middle of the twentieth century were still being used in some of the London orchestras. The superb pedal timpani available today make possible rapid changes of pitch that were once totally out of the question. This has led some conductors (and some players) to rewrite some of the eighteenth- and nineteenth-century repertoire by playing notes that *they think* the composer would have written had modern-day instruments been available—unfortunately, this almost invariably detracts from the piece rather than improving it!

The next development was the appearance of the plastic heads, which, like other innovations, were received with suspicion and hostility in some quarters when they first became available around 1960. The big plus of the plastic head, of course, is that it is virtually free from susceptibility to atmospheric change. The arguments for and against plastic or calf heads are very much a matter of personal opinion—at the present time it is sufficient to say that some of the top symphony orchestra timpanists opt for calf, some for plastic. My own view is that *some* works do sound better with calf heads, but certainly not all. In any case, timpani sound cannot be looked at in isolation—*all* the orchestral instruments have changed in the last century and consequently the whole orchestra sounds different. (Though the string *instruments* haven't changed, the strings themselves have.) There has, however, been a return to using genuine Baroque timpani with calf heads in the period orchestras and ensembles, which can only be applauded.

Today's timpanist will probably have a basic set of five drums at his or her disposal, usually around 32", 30", 28", 25", and 23" in diameter, with an overall range of virtually two octaves. The range of each drum is set entirely to suit the individual player's personal preference. The sticks or mallets may be of cane or may be rigid; the heads will have a covering of felt over a core of wood or other material—leather-covered and wooden sticks are also required. Again a huge variety of weights and types is available—for the most part the choice is left entirely to the player's own musicianship. The mainland European tradition of timpani playing has the smallest drum to the player's left and the largest on the right, as opposed to the non-European way (but including Britain) of largest to the left, smallest on the right. The explanations for this difference that I have heard seem to me to be rather tenuous and unconvincing: (*a*) that in the early days of timpani in the orchestra, double-bass players were sometimes assigned to play them, and as the strings on their own instruments have the lowest on the right, they automatically aligned the timpani similarly, or (*b*) that the mounted timpani played tonic and dominant, and as the right hand is usually the stronger of the two, the drum tuned to the tonic was placed to the right. But of course Britain has a long history of timpani in mounted bands and is with the U.S. rather than mainland Europe, so just how and why there are different traditions remains a mystery. Obviously in playing terms it is of no consequence whatsoever which way round the timpani are placed, but I find it intriguing that such differing traditions still exist—how fortunate we are that it doesn't extend to all the keyboard instruments! The timpanist is a key figure in the modern symphony orchestra, even though contemporary compositions do seem to concentrate more on the rest of the percussion section.

The choice of instrument available today is truly amazing, given the cost of a new set of timpani and the fact that, with reasonable care, they will last for many years. The shape of the shell is surprisingly variable. Which type of pedal action, and which shape of shell a player chooses, can only be personal preference—there is no right or wrong. There are fine, reputable players all over the world with a wealth of differing opinions.

Timpani based on the original Dresden design are now on offer from several manufacturers, obviously with all sorts of modifications and refinements, and drums of this type are

Premier Percussion

used by many of the world's top players. But parabolic shells and balanced-action pedal systems are also very popular with professionals, and the competition for their approval and custom is now quite intense. There are nine main manufacturers, most offering a comprehensive range, from fibreglass hand or pedal timpani ideal for school orchestras, through to the top-of-the-range models for professional players. The main manufacturers are as follows: Adams (Holland), Bergerault (France), Kolberg (Germany), LeFima (Germany), Ludwig (USA), Majestic (Holland), Pearl (Japan), Premier (Britain), Vancore (Holland) (brass bowls), and Yamaha (Japan). Kolberg, Lefima, and George Potter are the sources for Baroque timpani.

For those with a fascination with the way timpani have evolved over the centuries, Kolberg has now established a museum of percussion instruments.

Timp Toms

The name is given by some manufacturers to sets of three, four, or five tom-toms, mounted on a frame to be played by one player in the marching bands—the shell is usually slightly cut away at the front. It is a somewhat misleading name, since there is no resemblance to or connection with timpani.

Tom-Tom

A name loosely applied in the West to certain African and Eastern drums, but now generally applied to the cylindrical drum with wooden shells used in Western jazz and pop bands. Tom-toms are an essential part of the modern jazz drummers set, and are usually used in groups of three or more. They may be single- or double-headed, and range in size from around 18" to 10". The heads are now normally of plastic. The drums are usually mounted on stands or frames that are fully adjustable for height and angle. In jazz and pop, snare-drum sticks or brushes are the norm, and the tom-toms are combined with snare drum, cymbals, and a foot-pedal bass drum. Though these drums are occasionally used in the orchestra, concert toms are generally found to be more suitable.

See also Chinese Tom-Tom; Concert Toms; Rototom; Timp Toms

Tour Timps

Tour timps are a unique concept of pedal timpani from Marcus de Mowbray. There are inevitable comparisons with rototoms, since tour timps have no shell—just the drum head, frame, and pedal. While there is no suggestion that they will find acceptance in the professional symphony orchestra, they will certainly be of interest in other types of music, and of course musical education. At present tour timps are only made to order—normal sizes between 32" and 22", with additional sizes available on request. See Percussion Manufacturers and Suppliers.

Marcus de Mowbray

Triangle

In medieval times the triangle was somewhat similar to the sistrum, having loose metal rings added. Today it is merely a metal rod in the shape of a triangle, open at one corner, and is struck with metal beaters. The "ting" of the triangle is one of the most widely used percussion colours—the tone should be clear and silvery. In the orchestra several different sizes and weights are needed to cover all requirements, and nowadays a wide variety of beaters is expected to be available, from under ¼" to just over ½" thick. The player may hold the triangle with one hand (suspended from a loop of gut) and hold the beater in the other, or may employ a triangle stand so that he or she can play with two beaters. Many European and American orchestras apparently still hold the triangle for the classical repertoire, while most British bands seem to favour the triangle stand at all times: this is a matter of personal preference. Obviously the triangle is an unpitched instrument, though there is an element of pitch. Kolberg now produce triangles of different metals giving an amazing choice of timbre. Most composers write for a single triangle, but quite frequently now a score will require a set of three or four of graduated pitch, as in Messiaen's *Éclairs sur l'au-dela* and *Concert a quatre*, and Henze's *King of Harlem*. Triangles are of course widely

available, but many of the top professional players seem to opt for those from Black Swamp Percussion, Grover, or Kolberg.

Tsuzumi *see* Talking Drum

Tubaphone

Rarely seen now, the tubaphone is similar to the glockenspiel, but the notes are steel tubes instead of bars, the tone quality being a little rounder and mellower. Composers now seldom write for the tubaphone, and the only example that comes to mind is the "Dance of the Young Maidens" in Khachaturyan's Gayaneh ballet music. Kolberg have a two-octave tubaphone available, F4–F6.

See also Glockenspeil

Tubular Bells (British terminology for chimes) *see* Bells

Tumbas *see* Congas

Tuned Discs

Tuned discs are very similar to crotales, and are produced by Paiste in two-octave sets, C^6–C^8. By eliminating the raised central boss or nipple, the disc's sustaining qualities are made greater than those of crotales.

Tuned Gongs *see* Gongs

Tupan *see* Tapan

Turkish Crescent (*also known as* Jingling Johnny)

Fr. *chapeau chinois, pavilion chinois*; Ger. *Schellenbaum*; It. *albero sonagli*

The Turkish crescent, commonly known as a Jingling Johnny, comes from the janissary music of the Middle Ages, and consists of a pole carried at the head of a marching band with a decorative crescent, brass eagle, or plumes at the top and several rows of small bells underneath—the pole was raised up and let down in time with the pulse of the music. In my experience the one notable work using this is Berlioz's *Symphonie funebre*. It also appears in some nineteenth-century Italian opera scores as Mezza Luna'—literally, a half-moon or crescent. There are also some versions where the whole top part, decorations and bells, is mechanically rotated by the player. Unfortunately, though this may be more effective visually, it works to the detriment of the sound! Turkish crescents are sometimes mistakenly referred to as bell trees. They are still used to front some marching bands in Europe. Available from Kolberg.

Royal Military School of Music, Kneller Hall; photo by Raymond Fortt Studios

Turkish Zils

High-pitched finger cymbals. Widely available.

U

Udu Pot (*also known* as Pot Drum)

The udu pot comes from Nigeria, but there are similar drums to be found in various parts of the world. The pot is of clay,

AfroTon

with two holes—water is added to obtain the desired pitch. Bright sounds are obtained by slapping the body of the drum, deep bass sounds from slapping the holes. Available from AfroTon and others. Western versions are made by LP, Remo, and PJ Drums and Percussion.

V

Verdi Drum *see* Bass Drum

Verrophone *see* Glass Armonica

Vibraphone *or* Vibraharp

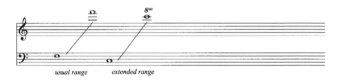

usual range   *extended range*

The vibraphone, more or less as we know it today, was invented in 1922 by Herman Winterhoff of the Leedy Drum Company in Indianapolis. Vibra*phone* was the trade name used by Leedy; vibra*harp* was the trade name used by Deagan, another of the big American drum manufacturers—vibraphone or vibes is the universal terminology in contemporary usage.

As a keyboard percussion instrument it is very widely used today in every type of music. The bars are of alloy and are arranged on the same level rather than with the accidentals raised up. Each note has a tube resonator—an axle runs through the line of resonators with a metal disc attached to the spindle under each bar. These discs, or fans as they are termed, are rotated by an electric motor and give the instrument its very distinctive vibrato. Early vibraphones often had clockwork motors, but electric power with a control to vary the speed of the vibrato is now universal. The instrument has a damper bar operated by a pedal of similar action to that of the piano, i.e., the pedal is depressed to *sustain* the sound. (Early models had the pedal action in reverse: the pedal was depressed to *stop* the sound. An encounter with one of these old instruments can be quite amusing!)

The vibraphone is now in common use in the orchestra, but quite frequently without the distinctive vibrato; composers should always indicate whether or not they require the vibrato, and if so indicate fast, medium, or slow. Without vibrato the vibraphone is, to all intents and purposes, a metallophone. The standard instrument is three octaves, F^3–F^6, but four-octave instruments, C^3–C^7, are readily available and now in everyday use.

Berg wrote for the four-octave instrument in his opera *Lulu* in the 1930s, and today's composers increasingly do so: virtually all the Henze repertoire require the four-octave range for example. Though the three-octave instrument is considered the most usual range, smaller two-and-a-half-octave versions were made at one time, chiefly for pit work; however, these no longer appear in any of the current catalogues.

A useful additional effect in the orchestra is achieved with a double-bass bow on the end of a bar. However, composers should use this sparingly. Obviously the player can only bow the end of the note protruding at the front or back of the instrument; the note then takes time to speak, and if both naturals and accidentals are required to be bowed in the same passage, then the player is probably better off using two bows. Also a fair amount of space is required to reach the accidentals.

The vibraphone is of course well known for its jazz connections, with names such as Lionel Hamptom, Milt Jackson, and Gary Burton acclaimed throughout the world. Gary Burton is additionally famed for his development of the grip for four mallets, which facilitates the playing of passages once thought impossible.

Three-octave vibraphones are available from Adams, Bergerault, Ludwig Musser, Premier, Studio 49, and

Premier

Yamaha. Adams and Yamaha also have a three-and-a-half-octave model, C^3–F^6; four-octave models, C^3–C^7, are available from Bergerault and Studio 49.

Vibraslap

The vibraslap is a sprung steel rod with an open-ended, wedge-shaped box containing loosely fastened rivets at one end; there is a wooden ball on the other end. When the ball is struck by the palm of the hand the rivets briefly vibrate, resonating in the wooden box. It makes a similar sound to the jawbone or quijade, but of course, unlike them, is totally reliable and consistent. The vibraslap initially came from LP Percussion; it is now a widely used effect in all types of music. Different sizes of vibraslap obviously give a differently pitched buzz.

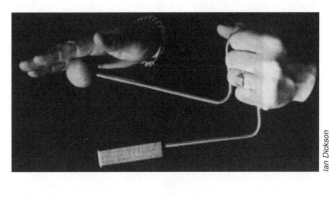

Ian Dickson

W

Waldteufel

The literal translation of Waldteufel is "forest devil." This is another friction drum, consisting of a small circular wooden shell with a single head, which has a cord fastened in the centre in similar fashion to the lion roar. In this instance the player holds the handle at the end of the cord and whirls the shell around; the resulting eerie whine of the air against the shell is somewhat reminiscent of the effect of the schwirrbogen or the Australian bull roarer. Available in three sizes, from Kolberg.

Washboard

The washboard occasionally appears in the percussion section today, but was a popular effect in the jazz bands of the 1920s, when the old household washboard was played by scraping thimbles across the bumpy metal surface. As a domestic implement it is now virtually obsolete, though washboards can still be found with a little determination. The sound is very metallic and rasping, rather more abrasive than the guiro, and I have known conductors ask for a washboard rather than a guiro in Stravinsky's *Rite of Spring*. PJ Drums and Percussion have three versions available, and

P.J. Percussion

Percussion Plus has one with a bell and woodblock added as additional effects.

Waterdrum (*also known as* Gourd in Water)

The waterdrum is from the African west coast and it consists of a large gourd bowl containing water with a smaller gourd floating upside down in it; the level of the water determines the pitch. It has a very warm, rich tone if played by hand, or a sharper sound if struck with a stick. Available from AfroTon, Kambala Percussion, Sabar Roots Percussion, and others.

Waterfall

Around forty small fibreglass shells strung together which simulate the sound of a waterfall. Produced by Meinl.

Water Gong

The water gong is the name given to the effect of dipping a vibrating gong or small tam-tam into water. As the gong is submerged a downward glissando is produced; and conversely, an upward glissando is produced as the gong is raised from the water.

John Cage employed the water gong in his *First Construction in Metal*, as did Henze in *King of Harlem*. The effect is somewhat heightened for the audience if the tank is of glass. A pedal device for lowering and raising the gong can also be an advantage.

Waterphone

The waterphone is a very strange-looking instrument devised by Californian percussionist Dick Waters. It consists of two metal pots welded together: a funnel is inserted, and different lengths of narrow brass tube welded around the edge. The container is half-filled with water, and when the brass rods are bowed or scraped all sorts of eerie, ethereal sounds are produced as the water slurps around inside. The waterphone has been utilized by a number of composers. Available from AfroTon, Kolberg, PJ Drums and Percussion, and others.

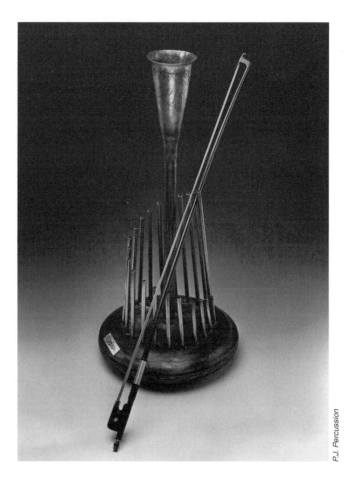

P.J. Percussion

Whip (*also* Slapstick)

Fr. *fouet*; Ger. *Peitsche, Holzklapper*; It. *frustra*; Sp. *fusta*

The whip consists of two thin, narrow pieces of wood, hinged at one end, very approximately 4" wide and 18" long. Handles or straps are attached for ease of playing (keeping fingers out of harms' way) and a realistic whipcrack is produced when the two surfaces strike sharply together. The slapstick is similar in effect, but has a handle at one end and a spring fitted with the hinge, so that only one hand is required. The slapstick is therefore often lighter than the two-handed whip, both in weight and volume. Both are widely available.

The whip is a very widely used effect, and almost always only one is required. If, however, a rapid rhythm is written, a double whip may be the only answer—two identical whips mounted on a board for one player. In Britten's *The Burning Fiery Furnace* a multiple whip of four different pitches is required.

P.J. Percussion

Whistle

Whistles of all types may be called for by composers. As with some other effects the word *whistle* covers many different sounds, from referee's whistle, police whistle, three-tone train whistle, and penny whistle to all the dozens of bird and game imitations. Composers should specify precisely the sound required. All the above are quite widely available.

See also Apito.

Wind Chimes

Bamboo: Fr. *bambou suspendu*; Ger. *Bambusrohre, Holzwindglocken*; It. *bambu sospeso*

Glass: Fr. *baguettes de verres*; Ger. *Glasstäbe*; It. *bacchete di vetro sospese*

Shell: Ger. *Muschel Windglocken*

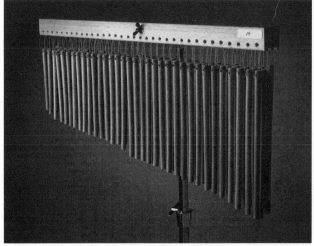

Kolberg Percussion

Wind chimes are particularly popular in the East, whether as door chimes or as decorations. For the percussionist they may be made of wood (usually bamboo), glass, glass tubes, shell, or metal tubes, and they are activated by hand (rather than the wind!). Wind chimes create a very abstract type of sound, but they do now contribute their extraordinary colour to many spheres of music, each type in its own unique way. Bamboo chimes (see figure) can also produce a very sharp 'thwack' when the bamboos are smacked together with both hands (an option not advisable with glass or shell!).

Wind chimes of all types are now used orchestrally by many composers, and are widely available, Asian Sound having a tremendous variety, particularly of the metal chimes. Glass chimes of quality are probably the most difficult to locate, but PJ Drums and percussion and Kolberg both have them.

Wind Machine

Fr. *machine à vent*; Ger. *Windmachine* or *Aeolophan*; It. *macchina a venti*; Sp. *maquina de viento*

The wind machine was first used as an effect in the theatre, but has long been used by composers. The machine is most usually in the form of a cylinder made up of wooden slats, with a sheet of canvas tightly held against the surfaces. The canvas is fixed, and when the cylinder is rotated the friction of the slats against the canvas produces a realistic wind sound. The pitch, volume, and sound intensity are governed by the speed of the rotating cylinder. Electric wind machines are also available, where the sound is usually produced by a fan, but of course the same subtleties are not possible. Also, the electric wind machine has a low-pitched but discernible hum which can be obtrusive in quiet passages. Examples of wind machine use may be found in Ravel's *Daphis and Chloe*, Richard Strauss's *Don Quixote*, and Vaughan

P.J. Percussion

Williams's *Sinfonia Antarctica*. In Bartók's opera *Bluebeard's Castle*, the wind machine does not appear in the percussion parts as it is normally used as a stage effect; however, in my experience most conductors *do* expect the percussion section to provide the effect, both for concert performances and recordings. Available from Kolberg and PJ Drums and Percussion.

Wine Glasses

Everyone is familiar with the unique "singing" of a wineglass when the rim is activated by a moistened finger. Different pitches are obtained by a combination of the size and thickness of the glass and the amount of liquid therein. An alternative effect is to use a cello bow rather than the finger. Percy Grainger extraordinarily required wineglasses or bowls for his *Tribute to Foster* sketched in 1913 as a birthday gift to his mother: the final scoring was in 1931. The chorus required glasses of C♯, D♯, A♯, F♯, and G♯, plus discordant or out-of-tune pitches for the second basses. Peter Maxwell Davies produces a beautiful effect at the end of his *Stone Litany*, with the soprano soloist, pianissimo marimba trill, and wineglasses in C^5 and E^5, and George Crumb writes for water-tuned crystal glasses B♭^{5}, D^6, E, G♯, and A in *Songs, Drones and Refrains of Death*. Available from Kolberg and others.

See also Glass Armonica

Wire Coils *see* Spring Coils

Wood Drum

Wood drums are exactly what the name implies: a wooden shell and a wooden head. A very useful additional sound, available in three sizes, 14", 12½", and 11½", all with the same height of 29½". From Schlagwerk Klangobjekte.

Woodblock

Fr. *bloc de bois*; Ger. *Holzblock*; It. *cassa di legno*; Sp. bois *de madera*

The conventional woodblock is a rectangular block of hardwood with a deep, narrow slit just underneath the top surface, and a similar slit in the underside. The centre and edge of the surface above either slit provide the best beating spots. Though woodblocks are presumed to be unpitched, the wide variety of sizes available does provide a great variation of pitch. Standard size is around 7" × 3", but larger blocks of up to about 12" × 3" or smaller ones down to 4½" × 2" are also available. The tone quality will vary tremendously according to the mallets employed, but the characteristic sound is usually sharp and brittle, much sharper than that of a temple block. Blocks made of other materials are now frequently used, usually with a slightly different tone quality. Tubular blocks are also encountered, though they are less popular. They consist of a tube of hardwood, hollowed out at each end to a different depth to give two different pitches; each end is also slit to increase the resonance.

Although woodblocks usually appear as an unpitched effect, Kolberg makes two chromatic octaves of woodblocks from C^5 to C^7. Bergerault makes a three-octave woodblock-xylophone. Otherwise they are widely available.

See also Mokubio

Kolberg Percussion

Wooden Agogo *see* Agogo Bells

Wooden Spoons *see* Spoons

X

Xylophone

Fr. *xylophone*; Ger. *Xylophon, Holz- und Strohinstumente*;
It. *silofono*; Sp. *xilofon*

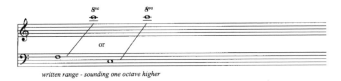

written range - sounding one octave higher

The xylophone has been known from ancient times, in various forms in many parts of the world. In Western orchestral music it first appeared in the nineteenth century, as an unresonated four-row tabletop instrument, very different in both sound and appearance to the xylophone we know today. However, the four-row instrument *does* still exist in parts of eastern Europe—a Romanian student at the Royal College of Music in London brought his own four-row with him as recently as 1998, and Lefima still have them in their catalogue (though I understand this to be a modified version). In their earliest form in the orchestra, the wooden bars were sometimes laid on straw ropes and their name reflects this: Richard Strauss writes for "Holz- und Strohinstrumente" in *Salome* and other works. In the early twentieth century there were also keyed xylophones, giving a xylophone sound, but operated by a piano-type keyboard. Bartók wrote for the keyed xylophone—"xilophone a tastiera"—in *Bluebeard's Castle*. I have never seen this instrument, nor have any of my colleagues, but I am assured that such an instrument does exist in a Budapest museum. The usual solution today is to use two players, each with a conventional xylophone.

The xylophone known to most contemporary percussionists has the wooden bars laid out keyboard style, with the accidentals raised. The bars are resonated, and the *written* range is usually three and a half octaves, F^3–C^7, or four octaves, C^3–C^7 (the xylophone sounds one octave higher than written). The best bars are of the Honduras rosewood,

though the difficulty of obtaining seasoned wood of sufficient quality has led to some manufacturers offering xylophones with bars made of synthetic materials. There is an inevitable difference in tone, which, in my opinion, makes them unsuitable for professional orchestras. As with the marimba, the rosewood notes need to be treated with care and kept as far as possible in an even temperature, avoiding close proximity to heating ducts or radiators. The characteristic sound of the xylophone is its dry, brittle tone—in Saint-Saëns's *Danse macabre* (1874), it is supposed to depict the rattle of the bones of the dead. Some people think that the resonators have taken the edge off the "nastiness" of the original, unresonated, instrument. Having only known the modern version, it is difficult for me to have an unbiased opinion, though some of the instruments with rosewood notes now on offer are, I feel, of dubious quality, especially in the lower register (due to a different tuning system). There is also divergence of opinion over the term *xylorimba*: some feel that this is merely a term for a larger xylophone, overlapping some of the marimba range, others, that a xylorimba is, by definition, an unresonated instrument. To most players it is a xylophone, pure and simple! To add to the confusion, in the 1930s there were also five-octave xylomarimbas which had xylophone tone quality but with the additional octave at the bottom. These instruments were very popular at the time with the many xylophone solo acts on radio and in the music halls, but dropped from popularity after the Second World War. The technical demands on the orchestral xylophonist have of course changed dramatically in the last fifty years—one had only to compare the writing of say, Stravinsky, to that of Boulez, Messiaen, or Tippett. (It is worth noting that Messiaen almost always wrote xylophone parts at pitch, rather than sounding an octave higher than written. Some of the Birtwistle works are similarly written.)

See also Balafon

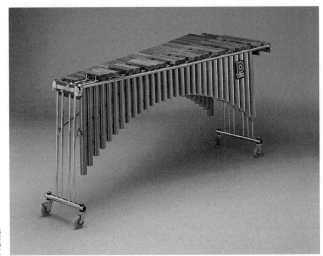

Xylosynth *see* Electronic Percussion

THE ORCHESTRAL PERCUSSION SECTION

It is worthwhile to ask ourselves precisely what we feel is the function of the percussion section in the orchestra. The orchestra is a large team, and to realize its full potential each player must be totally aware of *all* the other instruments, and ensure that his or her own contribution, both in tone quality and volume, enhances the overall sound. In the general core orchestral repertoire we percussionists have to acknowledge that for most of the time we are there for decoration, to point up a climax or underpin a crescendo; in the main orchestral repertoire we do not generally play the melody line or form part of the basic harmony. To me this means above all that we have to *listen*: Do I need harder sticks? Softer sticks? Is this the best woodblock to match the muted trumpets? Or, Is that *ppp* cymbal clash okay with the string chord, or would a cymbal slide sound better? Or, My *fff* cymbal crash is only *written* as a crotchet, but the brass chord lasts a whole bar so should I match it? Or, Are these the best bass drum sticks? Do I need more resonance? A "tighter" sound? More clarity? The best players are those with such questions constantly in their minds.

The second part of our raison d'être, in my view, is to reproduce the composer's ideas and wishes as accurately as possible. This may be especially difficult on those occasions, experienced by every player from time to time, when one feels absolutely zero rapport with the music, and/or the composer. That is when professionalism has to take over—though, if we are honest, we have all lapsed from time to time! The wise amongst us will try to refrain from making snap judgements, remembering all the music critics who have later had to eat their words! However, my many—mostly enjoyable—experiences of working with composers have given me a fascination for the great variety in their attitudes—what they *really* expect to hear from their percussion writing, and, crucially, what happens to their intentions after they die. In my experience, composers fall into three main categories:

1. The composer who knows *exactly* what he has written, and that is *exactly* what he expects to hear. This, I have to say, is very much the minority group! Examples of

composers in this group would include Boulez, Britten, and Messiaen. All three possessed a very discerning ear, and if in any doubt at all would be quite happily ask about anything of which they were unsure. Messiaen, I remember, had to see and approve every single percussion instrument before the first rehearsal of his opera *Saint Françoise d'Assise*. In *Des canyons aux étoiles* he could pick out any error in a great flurry of notes from a run of six temple blocks: "The second bar, second beat, fourth semiquaver, you played the third lowest block instead of the fourth." A chastening experience for any percussionist! Britten and Boulez also, though obviously worlds apart in their musical ideas, were always extremely discerning in the sounds they expected from the percussion section.

2. A very much larger group of composers are those who have a very relaxed, easygoing approach, some even changing their minds quite readily; I would even include the great Stravinsky in this group. He wrote three different versions of *Les Noces* before he was content, and several versions of both *Firebird* and *Petrushka*; his own recordings of *The Soldier's Tale* all differ quite widely in interpretation. William Walton's *Façade* is another case in point—when I asked Sir William what he intended by the instruction "on the wood," the reply was "Oh I don't mind what you do, dear boy—I did write it fifty years ago!"

Some composers give specific instructions either in error or because of lack of knowledge. In an early work by Peter Maxwell Davies the glockenspiel has the instruction, "sounding *one* octave higher than written." When questioned about this by the principal percussionist at a rehearsal many years later Max replied, "Oh no, I was very young, I didn't know what I was doing—just play it where you would normally play it"—how refreshingly honest! In contrast, Penderecki in his First Symphony writes for a binsasara, yet, at the first rehearsal (percussion sectional) he asked, "What are you going to use for a binsasara?" When I replied, "Well, I was going to use a binsasara" (having gone to considerable trouble to find one—it was around 1975) his reply was, "Oh, haven't you got anything else you could use?" I could only assume that the binsasara hadn't been available at an earlier performance and that he had preferred the substitute, whatever that had been, to his original choice, but of course no one had ever bothered to correct the orchestral parts.

3. There is also a school of composers who don't really want to hear their scores played with complete accuracy, but prefer a good attempt! In the early days of Harrison Birtwistle's career there was a nice apocryphal story of Pierre Boulez rehearsing a Birtwistle work with the BBC Symphony: apparently Harry was reputed to have stormed out of the studio muttering, "He's ruining it, he's ruining it—he's getting it all right!"

Xenakis, on being told that adding a percussionist would enable the part to be played with complete accuracy, would not even consider the idea—it was enough to see one player *attempting* to play what was written. Xenakis was one of those composers who specified diameters of cymbals and tamtams, which to my mind displays an extraordinary ignorance of the instruments. Every percussionist knows that diameter alone means nothing—it is very easy to find a 16" cymbal that is lower in pitch than an 18" one.

And after the composer has departed this world? Bartók is a prime example. The solo drum start to the second movement of his *Concerto for Orchestra*, for example: every single conductor that I have performed this piece with, from Bernstein to Boulez, Solti to Dorati, has wanted the second movement to be absolutely strict, "square" rhythmically. An American percussionist, Mike Quin, told me that he had studied with Simon Sternberg, who said that Bartók himself wanted the solo to be "jazzy"! The last movement of the same composer's *Music for Strings, Percussion and Celeste* is another case in point. Georg Solti showed me what he said was the original score, which showed the xylophone going into 8th note/quavers from the G♯ pick-up into the 3/2 bar in the last movement, rather than the 1/4 note/crotchets printed in the percussion part. However, when I asked Dr. Paul Sacher, who commissioned many of the Bartók works, he told me that Bartók *had* written 8th notes originally, but then changed his mind to the 1/4 notes after hearing the first performance. Which version is correct? Did Bartók change his mind, but only because the player at that time couldn't adequately manage the 8th notes? Of course, queries such as these cannot now ever be answered definitively one way or the other. Another instance is the end of Tchaikovsky's Fourth Symphony: did the composer *really* intend the final chord to be without the bass drum and cymbals, or was it merely a publisher's error?

I recently heard a student orchestra rehearsing Benjamin Britten's *War Requiem*, where one of the percussionists played an open, timpani-type roll on the tenor drum with snare-drum sticks. When I pointed out that Britten wanted a normal snare drum-type roll, the student replied that his professor had instructed him to play the open roll. All I could think was that poor old Britten was probably turning in his grave.

So, as time passes, it seems inevitable that, very frequently, the composer's deeply held ideas of how his or her work should sound will become more and more diluted.

Any list of twentieth-century composers whose orchestral writing has substantially contributed to the development of percussion would surely have to include the names of Bartók, Boulez, Grainger, Henze, Ives, Messiaen, Ravel, Shostakovich, Stravinsky, Tippett, and Varèse. If asked to pick out those who had the greatest influence, I think I would probably suggest Grainger, Varèse, Messiaen, and Boulez, though I'm quite sure many of my colleagues would come up with a different choice. Percy Grainger (1882–1961) was ahead of his time to a quite extraordinary degree, as is illustrated by just one work, *The Warriors*, written between 1913 and 1916 and premièred in 1917, that is to say it was commenced before the start of the First World War and before the invention of the vibraphone (1922). Given its date of composition, *The Warriors* is a most extraordinary orchestral work, and is especially so from a percussion standpoint. The large orchestra includes celeste, three pianos, two harps, timpani, and five percussion—playing xylophone, glockenspiel, snare drum, cymbals, bass drum, tambourine, gong, castanets, and woodblock—but it is the additional *nine* percussion parts (all optional) that are of such interest. The composer's instructions are very precise (see figure on page 63).

To present the work today, it would appear that two players could satisfactorily use two vibraphones (one a four-octave) for the "steel marimba," while still observing the composer's instruction for mallets. (His idea of the dulcitone as a substitute would appear in any case to be obsolete.) The "staff bells" are in fact handbells, and are of course readily available. The tubular bells have additional notes to the usual one-and-a-half-octave set.

Varèse (1883–1965) had a limited output of compositions, but this legacy has been very far-reaching. He apparently always said that he was not ahead of his time—it was the audiences who were behind! When one thinks of the booing that greeted the first performance of Stravinsky's *Rite of Spring* in 1912, he probably had quite a point. Of course the first thing that we percussionists associate with the name of Varèse is the number of players required: fifteen for *Hyperprism*, first performed in 1923, two timpanists and thirteen percussion for *Amériques* in 1925, two timpanists and fourteen percussion for *Arcana* in 1927, and thirteen percussion for *Ionisation* in 1933. The second thing is the instruments themselves, for in addition to the normal percussion instruments used in the 1920s were the Indian drum, lion roar, anvil, small and large ratchets, and siren (*Hyperprism*); siren and lion roar (*Amériques*); lion roar, horses' hooves, Chinese cymbal, and three tam-tams of graduated able until the 1970s, if I remember correctly. I vividly remember the first time I recorded *Ionisation* for the BBC in the early 1960s: the player strove in vain to "brake" the siren at the silent bar. The only remedy at that time was to record the passage twice, once with siren and again without, leaving the engineers to finalize matters.

Olivier Messiaen's legacy to the world of percussion is immense: his output was large, and most of his works not only employed several percussionists, but also considerably advanced both the technical and instrumental requirements. His compositions elevated percussion to hitherto undreamt-of heights, some of his works including percussion soloists: *La Transfiguration de Notre Seigneur Jésus-Christ* (1969) requires solo marimba, xylorimba, and vibraphone, and *Des canyons aux étoiles* (1971–4) solo xylophone and glockenspiel. Many of his other works also have very prominent parts for the keyboard percussion. The other significant feature of Messiaen's compositions is his use of chromatic cowbells (Almglocken), sets of crotales, two-octave sets of bells (chimes), graduated sets of gongs and tam-tams, and of course his liking for the geophone.

My first encounter with Pierre Boulez was when I was booked to play the xylophone in *Pli selon pli* around 1969. I had heard so much abut him, both as a conductor and a composer, that I was intrigued to find out for myself; some twenty-one rehearsals, two concerts, and seven recording sessions later (all in a fort-night!), I found I was hooked. The fact that Boulez knew exactly what he had written, spotted *every* (almost!) wrong note, and yet at the same time was always completely professional and a pleasure to work with (and he had a sense of humour) made him very much my sort of conductor, and the scope of the repertoire and the playing challenges made the offer of the principal percussion position with the BBC Symphony under his direction irresistible. Apart from the obvious technical demands of works such as *Le marteau sans maître* (1953–5), *Éclat-multiples* (1970), *Pli selon pli* (1959–62), and *Notations* (1980), it was the huge array of percussion instruments for *Pli* that made *such* an impression at the time; other percussionists came to that concert because they had heard so much about the piece, and wanted to see and hear this display for themselves. *Pli selon pli* requires a timpanist and eight percussion with the following instruments:

> two five-octave xylo-marimbas (or two four-octave xylophones and two marimbas)
> two vibraphones
> bell plates (two octaves)
> two-octave set bells (chimes) plus one and a half octaves with a low B♭
> three glockenspiels
> two bass drums
> seven suspended cymbals, one Chinese
> F^3–C^5 cowbells (Almglocken) plus six unpitched cowbells

pitch (*Arcana*); and medium, large, and extra large bass drums, high and low sirens, high and low anvils, keyed glockenspiel, and piano in *Ionisation*. Amazingly, given the number of players required, the BBC Symphony actually undertook a European tour with Pierre Boulez in 1972 that included *Amériques*. One can only imagine the premières of these works; sirens with an automatic cut-out facility are essential in some cases, but these were not avail-

six gongs
three tam-tams
two metal blocks
three snare drums
crotales
six pairs of bongos
one rototom
maracas
claves

This may not seem that extreme by today's standards, but in 1969 it was a great talking point. Of course at that time, availability of some of these instruments was also a real problem, solved in this instance because Pierre Boulez himself *owned* four octaves of Thai gongs, two octaves of bell plates, a two-octave set of bells (chimes), seven Paiste tam-tams between 18" and 40", and four and a half octaves of cowbells.

The percussion section was traditionally led by the timpanist, and astonishingly this is still the case in some professional orchestras. When orchestral percussion rarely ventured much beyond bass drum, cymbals, snare drum, triangle, etc., with the occasional few bars of glockenspiel, this was obviously a perfectly reasonable situation. However, I would suggest the percussion writing encountered today makes such a system quite ludicrous, and a separate position of principal percussion essential. One orchestra manager actually admitted to me (an unguarded moment I think!), that he thought the position of principal percussion now as important as that of the leader. The percussion section operates in a quite different way from the other parts of the orchestra, and the principal percussionist now has a wide-ranging role. He or she has to

1. (Usually) play the main part. This is likely to be fairly obvious in the standard orchestral repertoire, but in contemporary works several parts will frequently be of equal difficulty. The numbering of percussion parts is for convenience only, and does *not* automatically relate to the importance of the part (as would first, second, and third trumpet, for example).
2. Decide how many players are needed. This may be obvious if the composer has numbered percussion parts; however, if the composer has written all the percussion in score form it may take several hours to come up with a permutation that works.
3. Arrange for all the necessary instruments to be available, if necessary renting those not owned by the orchestra.
4. Allocate the parts to the other members of the section, matching players to instruments.
5. Oversee the overall percussion sound and decide on any necessary adjustments.

All of the above can now add up to a great deal of work before a note is played. In some professional orchestras the management will compromise on the number of percussion required, even though they would never dream of leaving out extra wind parts. On a tour some years back, we were in Seoul in South Korea and met the percussion section of one of the world's most famous symphony orchestras: we were astonished to find that there was one timpanist and three percussionists in the orchestra, and if they needed more players the librarian and a back-desk cellist made up the numbers. When they asked how we operated, they were equally astonished when I said that if the score required twelve percussion we engaged twelve percussionists. In my experience composers themselves are frequently incapable of assessing the number of percussionists required. The first performance of Copland's *Music for a Great City* (in about 1963) is but one example: the composer himself told the London Symphony Orchestra management that four percussionists would be required; I looked at the parts and said six players were needed. There were never more than four instruments playing at a given point, but, if they all play up to the end of a given bar and the following bar starts with different instruments, the only solution may be more players (this obviously depends on the instruments involved). In contrast, some composers give their percussion parts a great deal of thought and provide very specific instructions.

The principal percussionist also needs to be looking ahead all the time, monitoring the advance schedule to avoid embarrassing situations. Some contemporary scores require very considerable stage area for the percussion, and by no means all concert halls are suitable. I well remember my first European tour having just joined the BBC Symphony, with Berio work that required a very large percussion section (see figure). We were scheduled to play in Geneva,

The percussion requirements for George Crumb's *Star-child*

where it took just one glance at the platform to tell the orchestra management that the piece was totally impossible in that context. I found it astonishing that they had no prior knowledge of the stage dimensions. The result was the embarrassment of cancelling the Berio work, a wasted journey for the soloist Cathy Berberian, and an unexpected bonus night off for several percussionists.

Looking back on all my years with orchestras, I can see that the instruments have, generally, improved beyond belief. The general standard of playing technique has also improved immeasurably. Standards of musicianship, however, are another subject altogether: we have many superb percussionists whose "feel" for the music is unquestionable, but, for my taste, rather too many who evidently have little sympathy with the music they are playing. A short time ago I found myself with an orchestra playing a suite from *Swan Lake* and was introduced to a player who I hadn't come across before, who proceeded to try and reproduce a kit bass drum sound at full volume on the orchestral bass drum. To me, at any rate, this fell woefully short of the standards we have come to expect. One unmusical percussionist can do so much damage.

THE PERCUSSIONIST AS SOLOIST AND IN ENSEMBLES

Though there have long been works for solo timpani and/or percussion, no one can deny the huge changes in both repertoire and performers in the last forty years. We have gone from the avant-garde material of Stockhausen and Xenakis to more mainstream works such as H. K. Gruber's *Rough Music*, Joseph Schwantner's *Concerto for Percussion and Orchestra*, and James MacMillan's *Veni, Veni, Emmanuel* which has now received more than 200 performances (Evelyn Glennie being the soloist on over 130 occasions). In the 1960s and 1970s percussion ensembles were very much in vogue, led mainly by Les Percussions de Strasbourg in France and Nexus in Canada, both groups attracting the attention of a variety of composers. Olivier Messiaen was but one leading composer who recognized the importance and lasting contribution of the Strasbourg group—"They are pioneers in the evolution of percussion in contemporary music. Without them there would be far fewer works written for percussion, and fewer percussionists"—accurate words indeed. Of course, as we have seen, Messiaen himself was certainly a great contributor to the percussion scene, and I for one would certainly acknowledge his very considerable contributions to my salary cheques! The percussion ensemble is still an important part of the musical scene, with both the aforementioned groups still well to the fore, and the likes of Ensemble Bash in Britain making their mark, both with contemporary works and also with some stunning performances of traditional West African drumming, the product of several African tours.

The other important, and relatively new, part of the solo percussion scene that has to be recognized is of course the appearance of the marimba as a solo instrument. On film sessions in the 1960s we mainly used three-octave instruments, but the marimba's astonishing rise in popularity means that today's soloists use five-octave instruments. So much was written for the marimba in the last quarter of the twentieth century; the Steve Weiss Catalogue alone has around 600 unaccompanied marimba works, and a small sample of the most popular works would have to include Paul Creston's *Marimba Concerto*, Mitchell Peters's *Yellow after the Rain*, Gordon Stout's *Mexican Dances*, Paul Smadbeck's *Rhythm Song*, Keiko Abe's *Michi and Variations on Japanese Children's Songs*, and Minory Miki's *Marimba Spiritual*.

Probably the first work featuring percussion as a solo instrument was the Philidor brothers' *March for Two Kettledrummers*, composed in 1685. Each player has two drums, the first in G and C, and the second the E and G above—a short but very effective piece. A century later, in 1785, came *Concerto for Eight Timpani and Orchestra* by Johann Carl Fischer. But for many years after, the timpanists' and percussionists' moments of solo glory were very few and far between.

One of the first, if not *the* first, percussion concerto was written by Darius Milhaud in 1929. A short, "fun" piece, the instruments listed for the soloist are four timpani, tam-tam, caisse claire, caisse roulante, tambourin provençal, tambourine, ratchet, whip, castanets, crash cymbals, woodblock, cowbell, suspended cymbal, triangle, and pedal bass drum with cymbal attached. Milhaud also later (around 1947) wrote a concerto for marimba, vibraphone, and orchestra; this requires a very adept four-stick technique, and was certainly rather ahead of its time. Stravinsky's *Soldier's Tale*, written in 1918, was one of the first significant chamber works to use percussion. It was written as a stage work, but unfortunately today it appears most frequently as just a concert suite. The percussion instruments are listed as triangle, tambourine, two caisse claire without snares, two tambours, one with snares and one without, and a bass drum with cymbal attached. Though much has been written about the correct order of the drums (some of the original printed part being a nightmare for the player to interpret), the type of drums, which sticks, etc., I am firmly of the opinion that Stravinsky himself merely wanted an early drumkit type of sound, but wasn't too sure of just how to put it down on paper. To my mind, three recordings—1932 in Paris, 1954 in New York, and 1961 in Los Angeles, *all conducted by Stravinsky*—confirm this (with apologies to my late esteemed colleague, James Blades, who edited the percussion part for the new edition, published in 1987). The concert suite today is of course usually unconducted. Any percussionist who has enjoyed playing *The Soldier's Tale* will, I am sure, also enjoy playing the short solo percussion work

The Love of L'Histoire by Charles DeLancey, which was written in 1973 as a tribute to Stravinsky. The way the composer weaves in the very recognizable strands of the original work is extremely cleverly done and so very effective (see figure).

Most percussionists have some knowledge of Bartók's *Sonata for Two Pianos and Percussion* (1938), even if they have never played the work themselves. The sonata is indisputably another milestone work in percussion history, with the two percussionists treated as equals and not merely accompanists. (There is also an orchestral version, the piano parts slightly changed from the original, the percussion remaining the same. To my ear, the original two piano/two percussion version is very much more effective.)

Dedicated to the memory of Igor Strawinsky, and to all percussionists who love playing the "Batterie" in L'HISTOIRE DU SOLDAT.

The Love Of L'Histoire

MULTIPLE PERCUSSION SOLO

Charles DeLancey

First page of "Love of L'Histoire" (Mitchell Peters)

A work seldom heard is *L'Envol d'Icare* by Igor Markevitch, also written for two pianos and two percussion. My personal experience of Igor Markevitch was as a world-renowned conductor, and it was only when recording this work many years later that I learnt that, back in the 1920s, he was also very highly regarded as a composer—a Pierre Boulez of his day, one might say. *L'Envol d'Icare* was in fact written in 1929, thus pre-dating the Bartók sonata by some nine years. Though Markevitch does not employ any tuned percussion, the similarities in the scoring are very evident. One percussionist needs timpani, triangle, tambourine, bass drum, and caisse claire, and the other has piccolo snare drum, military snare drum, caisse roulante, bass drum, triangle, suspended cymbal, and tam-tam. The similarities are not confined to the instruments, for the use of the percussion by Bartók is in very similar mode, and the Markevitch work makes an ideal companion to go with the sonata. As always, the percussionists in this type of chamber work must remember to keep their contribution in proportion to the other instruments; it is not a percussion concerto.

A solo percussion work that has received many performances is Karlheinz Stockhausen's *Zyklus*. I once heard this work described as a masterpiece, but I would describe it as an interesting study—no more, no less.

Its popularity in the 1960s and 1970s was, I feel, largely due to the shortage of material for solo percussion. Of course this situation has changed radically in the last twenty years with the appearance of a number of very effective works. In *Zyklus* the player is given a huge amount of freedom in performance, but is also given a large page of very explicit instructions, some of which are bizarre to say the least. The snare drum, for instance, is to be very high pitched, but if the snares buzz too much because of the other instruments, then the drum should be without snares—a completely different sound. It is difficult to imagine Shostakovich or Ravel giving this sort of instruction! The Player can also start at any chosen point in the work, and must then proceed through and finish with the first stroke of the page that includes the starting point. One of London's top percussionists was once told by Stockhausen that he would have to study with him personally for three months before he could even contemplate a performance.

Luciano Berio's *Circles*, written in 1960 for female voice, harp, and two percussion, is, in my opinion, rather more effective. The percussion requirements are rather extensive:

Player 1 has sandpaper blocks, Mexican bean, three woodblocks, log drum, marimba, four bongos, three tom-toms, two timpani, glass and wood wind chimes, three triangles, three suspended cymbals (the lowest being a sizzle), three tam-tams, celeste, guiro, five cowbells, bells in B^3, C^4, D, E, F, and A$\flat$, lujon, hi-hat, finger cymbals, and talking drum (this

appears in the score as "tabla", but the composer had a change of mind).

Player 2 requires three triangles, three suspended cymbals (the middle one being a sizzle), hi-hat, crash cymbals, glass wind chimes, vibraphone, glockenspiel, four Chinese gongs in F$\sharp$, A, B$\flat$, E^4, tambourine, bongos, snare drum, three tom-toms, two congas, pedal bass drum, five temple blocks, maracas, xylophone, and tabla (again, it is the talking drum that is actually required).

In addition, the singer needs finger cymbals, glass and wood wind chimes, and claves (usually provided by the percussionists).

This sort of percussion writing, apart from its very obvious technical demands, places great responsibilities on the players in terms of ensemble.

Though the repertoire is widening all the time, as is the number of percussion virtuosi, the three works mentioned at the beginning of this chapter, the Gruber, Schwantner, and MacMillan, are all now recognized as mainstream orchestral concerti. The Gruber *Rough Music* was the first of these, written in 1982 and premièred in 1983 in Vienna by Gerald Fromme with the ORF Symphony Orchestra conducted by Lothar Zagrosek. The soloist requires

marimba, three-octave vibraphone
two suspended cymbals, two Chinese cymbals, hi-hat
bongos, five tom-toms, snare drum, large orchestral bass drum, and pedal bass drum
two vibraslaps (mounted), whip
three small cowbells, three large cowbells, and chromatic cowbells B^4–C$\sharp^6$
mouth siren, mounted tambourine
four timpani (range required D^3–C^4)

This is a very effective *tour de force* for the soloist, and great fun to play.

Joseph Schwantner's *Concerto for Percussion and Orchestra* was commissioned by the New York Philharmonic for its 150th anniversary season. It received its première in January 1995 in Lincoln Center, New York, the soloist being the orchestra's principal percussionist, Christopher Lamb. The composer's tribute to his first soloist speaks volumes: "His astonishing virtuosity and compelling musicianship proved to be an endless wellspring of inspiration that helped shape and propel the flow of my musical ideas." This concerto has one crucial difference from the other two works: while all three orchestrations include an orchestral timpanist, the Schwantner alone also includes three percussion, and these three players all have crucial roles to play, their parts being interwoven with that of the solo percussionist. The solo part requires two setups, one at the back near the orchestral percussion, and one front of stage in a normal solo position. The soloist plays the first movement at the back, the second front of stage, and at the commencement of the third movement slowly progresses to the back again while playing the shekere. The instruments required are

> *Back position*: amplified marimba (normal range), xylophone, two octaves crotales, orchestral bass drum, two tom-toms, timbales, bongos.
>
> *Front of stage*: vibraphone, one octave crotales, water gong, orchestral bass drum, tenor drum, two suspended cymbals, two triangles, rute, shekere, cowbells in D^4, F, F♯, G♯, A, B, C^5, and E♭.

Again, this is a superb vehicle for the soloist to show off his or her skills, finishing with a dazzling solo cadenza. (This was the work played by Adrian Spillett to win the 1998 prestigious BBC Television Young Musician Award, not merely a personal triumph for Adrian, but also a triumph for percussion in the wider sense.)

James MacMillan's *Veni, Veni, Emmanuel* was first performed at the Royal Albert Hall, London, in August 1992, with Evelyn Glennie as soloist and with the Scottish Chamber Orchestra conducted by Jukka-Pekka Sarasate. The solo part requires

> Five-octave marimba, three-octave vibraphone
> Six gongs, two woodblocks, six temple blocks, log drum
> Two cowbells, large suspended cymbal and sizzle cymbal
> Two bongos, two congas, six tom-toms, two timbales, pedal bass drum
> Large and small tam-tams, mark tree
> Bells (perferably 2") in E^4, F sharp, G, A, B, and D^5

Veni, Veni has proved to be very popular with both percussionists and audiences, and has now received well over 200 performances. These three concertos alone demonstrate the huge advances percussion has made in the last fifty years.

An unusual but very effective work for solo percussion group and orchestra is Toru Takemitsu's *From Me Flows What You Call Time*, written for Nexus, and premièred by them at Carnegie Hall, New York, in October 1990 with the Boston Symphony conducted by Seiji Ozawa. The scoring for the five solo percussionists is extraordinarily imaginative, with an emphasis on instruments from the East:

> *Player 1*: glockenspiel, vibraphone, lead steel pan G♯^{3}–C♯^{6}, two crotales in B♭^{4} and E^5.
>
> *Player 2*: seven Pakistan Noah bells D♭^{4}, E♭, G, B♭, E♭^{5}, G♭ and A♭; five Thai gongs G^2, d♭^{3}, E, A, B♭; crotales, F^4–C^5, two Japanese temple bells, A^3 and F^4, to be used on large timpani; six Chinese winter gongs, A^3, b♭, C^4, D♭, E♭, and E; a pair of crotales in C^5, anklung in C^4, and a darabuka.
>
> *Player 3*: a pair of crotales in C♯^{5}, five Almglocken (unspecified pitch); log drums in F♯^{3}, A, B♭, C^4, D, F, F♯, and G♯; five rototoms and anklung in F♯^{4}.
>
> *Player 4*: a pair of crotales in F♯^{5}, glockenspiel, marimba, three tam-tams (high, medium, and low), three suspended cymbals (high, medium, and low), three Chinese cymbals (very high, medium, and medium-low), anklung in E^4.
>
> *Player 5*: a pair of crotales in A^4, glockenspiel, marimba, anklung in G sharp^4, and six Japanese temple bells on two timpani, E♭^{4}, B and A♭^{5}, G♭^{4}, F^5, and C^6.

In addition there are tiny bells hanging from different-coloured ribbons strung right across the auditorium.

Percussionists of the twenty-first century now have tremendous opportunities, both in solo and ensemble works, to make real music, and communicate with their audiences to a degree once thought impossible. As just one example of what is now on offer, Adrian Spillet (mentioned above in the Schwantner concerto) now has a percussion group with the name 4-Mality—the musicianship, technical brilliance, and sheer entertainment value all help to raise the profile of percussion to new levels.

WRITING AND PUBLISHING
MUSIC FOR PERCUSSION INSTRUMENTS

As a player one becomes very aware of the composers and arrangers who write effectively for percussion, and of those whose writing is comparatively ineffective. But I readily acknowledge that percussion today does present composers with all sorts of challenges and complications that they do not experience with other instruments. This short section is designed to list a few points that composers may find constructive.

If writing for several players, one of the decisions for the composer is whether to write a percussion score and leave it to the principal percussionist to decide how many players are necessary, or to write separate parts for each player. Obviously there is no right or wrong in this—it is the composer's choice, sometimes dictated by the scoring, sometimes not. Some points are applicable whichever course is taken, and though the following may be glaringly obvious to some, all too frequently composers are unaware of the problems.

1. Bear in mind that to make the best/most suitable sound on any percussion instrument means being able to use the right mallets. For example, it is not possible to come straight off a xylophone run onto a tam-tam beat, or to use four mallets on the vibraphone and continue without a break on a glockenspiel or xylophone.
2. To play an effective snare-drum roll it is necessary to use snare-drum sticks—no substitutes are possible.
3. Changing mallets, turning a page, putting snares on or off, picking up or setting down crash cymbals or finger castanets—all these take time, even if only two or three seconds.

4. Tubular bells/chimes: if these are only required for an occasional note here and there, the positioning of the bells and the score is not of any great consequence; if the part is continuous and of any complexity, then the player probably needs to be standing at the bells with the score placed centrally above.
5. For the percussionist to fulfill his or her job of faithfully reproducing the composer's wishes, the instructions on the part need to be as explicit as possible.
6. If, subsequent to writing the piece, the composer has a change of mind about the percussion part in any way at all, *please* ensure that the publisher properly updates the parts *and* score. This can save a great deal of time, trouble, and misunderstanding and is very much in the composer's own interests!
7. Always indicate whether the vibraphone should be with or without motor, and, if vibrato is required, whether it is slow, medium, or fast.
8. If the percussion has been written in score form and is of any complexity, it will usually be worthwhile to employ an experienced player to advise the publisher on the best way to divide and present the percussion parts.
9. Although it may appear to be stating the obvious, if the percussion is printed in score form, the order of the instruments on the page must be constant throughout the piece.
10. Use abbreviations of instrument names rather than symbols.

PERCUSSION IN EDUCATION

The huge expansion of percussion generally in the second half of the twentieth century is certainly matched, if not surpassed, by the use of percussion instruments at all levels of education, and its proven value in the field of music therapy. A seemingly endless array of instruments and effects suitable for playschool onwards is now available—all a very long way from the very basic instruments of my own childhood. Today there are all sorts of brightly coloured musical toys shaped as animals or fruit—even a tuned percussion instrument shaped as a zebra! There are also copies of some of the more unusual ethnic instruments, such as rainmakers, Burma bells, Chinese bell trees, and agogo bells. For the youngest children, for example, one catalogue has tambourines, maracas, handbells, ocarinas, slide whistles, and castanets, all shaped and decorated as animals, with all sorts of shakers similarly appearing as fruit. Hence the tambourines have names, such as Orange Bear, Black Penguin, and Brown Koala, handbells are Yellow Monkey or Green Frog, the ocarina is Yellow Duck, the slide whistles are blue and pink Mynah birds, the shakers are Red Apple, Lemon, or Banana, and castanets are Blue Whale, Yellow Duck, White Panda, etc.—all very imaginative, and sure to appeal to very small children. The zebraphone is also designed to appeal to that age group—a freestanding sound centre with thirteen bars/notes, and other effects, such as scrapers and castanets, built in. For the next stages of children's musical development, boxed sets for a whole class are available. A typical key Stage 1 set consists of

two pairs of finger cymbals
one eight-note chime bar
two tambourines
eight chime bars with beaters
two handbells
one woodblock with beater
two sets of castanets
one stick handbell
four triangles
one tone block with beater
one agogo bell
one pair maracas

A key Stage 2 set might be made up of

two pairs 6" marching cymbals
two pairs 8" marching cymbals
two pairs claves
two pairs castanets
pair maracas
8" triangle and beater
rhythm cabaca
agogo bell
tambourine
eight-note chime bar set
tulip block
set of handbells
10" drum with beater
twenty-five-note glockenspiel

Chime bars are available both singly and in sets, the idea being that they can be used individually, one per child, or assembled together as a small keyboard instrument.

Thus a child can build up to a complete scale, F and G major scales being popular as a starting point because they are most likely to correspond to children's singing voices. Chime bars are now available in several octaves, and are made in metal, wood, and substitutes such as resophen. Two other novel ways of presenting them are: (a) as a ladder, so that the notes of the scale correspond to the rungs of the ladder as they progress upwards; (b) with each note having a handle and beater built into one unit, so that each player can have one or several bars, and contribute much in the same way as handbell ringers—the bars being black or white like those on a piano keyboard.

No section on music in education would be complete without mention of Carl Orff (famous as the composer of *Carmina Burana*) and his brainchild Orff Schulwerk. It was in 1932 that Orff started putting forward entirely new ideas for musical education, the aim being to familiarize children with music from an early age, with attention to rhythm, melody, harmony, and improvisation. The Orff instruments are designed with all this in mind, and the obvious success of the system means that Orff Schulwerk instruments are now produced by several companies and are sold worldwide. One of the inspirations for Orff's vision was a present of a "Kaffir piano," an African instrument in the form of a xylophone, built from a small rectangular box. It had the inscription "10,000 Bretterstifte" (wooden pegs), printed on the side, there were twelve wooden bars tied together with string across the open top of the box, and it was apparently played with a single beater. According to Orff, the sound was amazingly good, and he decided that he had found the model for his work. Schulwerk instruments now include boxed versions of xylophones, glockenspiels, and metallophones in a great variety of ranges, and in both diatonic and chromatic scales. There is also a huge range of drums and effects, all specifically designed for music in education.

Percussion instruments to suit older children are also now provided to a hitherto undreamt-of standard. Pedal timpani and all the keyboard percussion are available at very realistic prices. Drumkits, of course, are available in many forms; obviously there are many more students wanting to learn kit drumming than orchestral percussion, and most senior schools now have a peripatetic teacher who can cover both kit and percussion. Companies such as Adams even have a junior marimba, designed for children aged 6 to 16. The photograph on the front of their leaflet shows the marimba together with a child's bicycle, a football, and badminton racquets!

Steel bands are another way of introducing the enjoyment of music and music-making to children, and they now have their own arrangements, concerts, and competitions and achieve extraordinarily high playing standards.

A relatively new development is the recognition that some percussion instruments can be of great value in assisting people with learning difficulties, both mental and physical. Accordingly there are now custom-built instruments that can help in this—afuches, bell trees, tambourines, etc.—all mounted on solid boards with non-slip feet, and "sound stations"—various different percussion effects all mounted together in special units. The benefit of music therapy in helping some of the less fortunate in society is now widely accepted, and percussion instruments play a large part in this.

Companies specializing in educational percussion include De Gouden Brug BV, Marcus de Mowbray (tour timps—unique fold-away pedal timpani), Percussion Plus, Sonor, and Studio 49 Royal Percussion. Addresses and contact numbers are all listed in the section on percussion manufacturers.

PERCUSSION MANUFACTURERS AND SUPPLIERS

The availability of some percussion instruments and accessories can vary tremendously. To buy a drumkit or a set of congas is very straightforward in most parts of the world, but some other percussion instruments can present great problems. If I need to buy a glass armonica, two octaves of anklung, or a kring, where do I start to look? This list of manufacturers and suppliers can obviously only be a token gesture, but I hope it will provide some valuable information. As will become apparent to the reader, small companies can have a very large impact on the overall percussion scene. Obviously, the information given here is very largely dependent on the cooperation received from the various manufacturers. So, apologies for any glaring omissions, but the fault is not necessarily mine! I have also included two of the world's largest stockists of percussion music and method books: Southern Percussion in England, and Steve Weiss Music in the U.S.

For professional orchestras or opera houses to own instruments to cover every percussion possibility is obviously not a viable option. Therefore most, though certainly not all, countries also have percussion rental companies to cover the more unusual instruments and effects.

Adams

Adams Musical Instruments was established at the end of the 1960s by André Adams, and is based at Thorn in The Netherlands. Adams has now become one of the world's leading companies, manufacturing and developing percussion instruments.

From lightweight pedal timpani that are both very easy to transport and very reasonably priced—ideal for schools and bands—through to top-of-the-range professional timpani and concert marimbas, the influence of Adams on the world of percussion is now immense. Apart from their quality, a great deal of thought has been given to the adaptability and portability of the instruments. Hence the playing height of the keyboard instruments is adjustable (a refinement now copied by other companies), as are the tubular bells both for height and range. There are even junior marimbas designed for players from 6 to 16 years.

Adams now manufactures a very comprehensive range of pedal timpani, xylophones (three and a half and four octaves), marimbas (four and a third, four and two thirds, and five octaves), tubular bells/chimes (one-and-a-half- and two-octave sets), bell plates (four octaves), vibraphone (three octaves), orchestral bells/glockenspiel (up to three and a half octaves), concert bass drums, temple blocks, and a range of mallets.

Adams Musical Instruments
Casino 29
6017 BS Thorn
The Netherlands

tel 31–(0)475–562833
fax 31–(0)475–563328

website: www.adams.nl

AfroTon

AfroTon was founded in 1986 by Michael Röttger in Frankfurt. Fascinated by the diversity of African rhythms and instruments, he spent some six months in West Africa in 1985, and his ideas of bringing African musical culture to Europe were conceived.

As Michael himself says, "The joy of living, which is so characteristic of African music, cast a spell on me." In the fourteen years since AfroTon started, this has now developed to become a vital source for ethnic instruments from many countries, not only from the African continent: djembes, waterdrums, bougarabous or grass harps from Africa, didgeridoos from Australia, darabukas from Egypt and anklung from Indonesia; the extent of the AfroTon catalogue is quite amazing.

AfroTon
Russelheimer Strasse 22
60326 Frankfurt
Germany

tel 49–(0)69–97–30–31–0
fax 49–(0)69–97–30–31–21

American Drum Manufacturing Co.

The American Drum Manufacturing Company was born in 1950, the brainchild of Walter Light, the esteemed timpanist of the Denver Symphony Orchestra (as was his father before him). Apparently, Walter Light Jr. was unhappy with the instruments available after WWII and decided to build his own, based on German Dresden-style drums. Half a century later, the company is still owned and operated by the Light family (Walter having died in 1979) and still produces world-class custom-built timpani.

American Drum Manufacturing Ltd.
P.O. Box 40403
Denver, CO 80204
USA

tel 1–303–722–3844
fax 1–303–722–3025

email: comments@americandrum-w-light.com
website: www.americandrum-w-light.com

Asian Sound

The history of Asian Sound is a fascinating example of the development of the percussion world. As a percussion soloist and composer, Michael Ranta went to Japan in 1979, moving to Taiwan in 1972. The original occasional request from friends and colleagues for help in locating ethnic percussion instruments grew to such an extent (with a request, amongst others, from Carroll Sound in New York for 500 temple blocks), that he felt compelled to start a company to cope with the demand. By 1976 this was in partnership with the Feedback Studio Cologne and Michael was travelling around Japan, Korea, Taiwan, Thailand, and the Philippines looking for sources of quality instruments. In 1979 Asian Sound was set up as a separate company and has widened its scope to such a degree that the catalogue now includes percussion instruments from all the countries of the East, including tam-tams, cymbals, gongs, tom-toms, wind chimes, chromatic gongs, anklung, handbells, temple bells, and much, much more. In addition there are the chromatic Bavarian cowbells and other percussion instruments with origins rather closer to home. Asian Sound is another key player in the contemporary percussion scene.

Asian Sound
Venloer Strasse 176
D-50823 Cologne
Germany

tel 49–(0)221–952–2300
fax 49–(0)221–52–64–83

Avedis Zildjian

Zildjian is the most famous name in the history of cymbal making, with an extraordinary history dating back to 1623. According to folklore, the original Avedis Zildjian, an alchemist working on the outskirts of Constantinople, discovered a process that strengthened a mixture of approximately 80 percent copper and 20 percent tin to produce a cymbal that was both musical and durable. The Turkish word for cymbals is "zil;" "dji" denotes smith or maker, and "ian" is the Armenian suffix meaning "family" or "son of," hence Zildjian. It appears that this original secret process was then handed down orally from generation to generation of the Zildjian family. In the 1920s a disagreement in the family led to Avedis Zildjian setting up a factory near Boston, Massachusetts, leaving the other part of the family still making cymbals in Istanbul. This Avedis died in 1979, leaving the business to his two sons Armand and Robert. Further disagreements between the two brothers led to another split, Robert Zildjian leaving to set up the Sabian Cymbal Company in 1982.

Avedis Zildjian remains one of the main world players in cymbal making, producing all types of cymbal, plus tam-tams and gongs (both made in China), two octaves of crotales, plus Burma bells, finger cymbals, metal castanets, etc.

Avedis Zildjian Company
22 Longwater Drive
Norwell, MA 02061
USA

tel 1–791–871–2200
fax 1–781–871–9652
international fax 1–781–871–9313

International Representative Office

The Barn
Handpost Farmhouse
Maidens Green
Berks, RG42 6LD
England

tel 44–(0)1344–885560
fax 44–(0)1344–885559

website: www.zildjian.com

Mike Balter Mallets

Mike Balter is a renowned percussionist/drummer in Chicago, and the comprehensive range of mallets that bears his name is popular with professional players worldwide.

Mike Balter Mallets
15 E. Palatine Road, Suite 116

Prospect Heights, IL 60070
USA

tel 1–847–541–5777
fax 1–847–541–5785

e-mail: info@mikebalter.com
website: www.mikebalter.com

Bergerault

The French company Bergerault was founded in 1932 by Albert Bergerault. Today, the catalogue includes three- and four-octave vibraphones, four-, four-and-a-half- and five-octave marimbas; three-and-a-half- and four-octave xylophones; two-and-a-half- and three-octave glockenspiels; with or without pedal; one-and-a-half- and two-octave bells/chimes, a full range of timpani; and three octaves of woodblocks laid out as a xylophone. They also make a range of school instruments, including glockenspiels, metallophones, and xylophones.

Bergerault Percussion Contemporaines SA
Route de Ferrière
BP2–37240 Ligueil
France

tel 33–(0)16–47–59–0459
fax 33–(0)16–47–92–0679

e-mail: percussion@bergerault.com
website: www.bergerault.com

Black Swamp Percussion

Black Swamp Percussion was founded in 1994 by Eric Sooy, and in a very short space of time has acquired an enviable reputation for the quality of its concert percussion, including snare drums, tambourines, triangles, castanets, woodblocks, and mallets. Black Swamp instruments are now used by many of the top players and orchestras.

Black Swamp Percussion
13493 New Holland Street
Holland, MI 49424
USA

tel 1–616–738–3190
fax 1–616–738–3105

website: www.blackswamp.com/html/about.html

Bosphorus

Bosphorus is a company producing all types of cymbal, both in Turkey and the U.S.

Bosphorus Turkey
Galipdede Cad. No. 83
Tunel-Istanbul
Turkey 80050

tel 90–212–249–38–67
fax 90–212–249–27–37

Bosphorus USA
6020 Dawson Blvd, Suite F
Norcross, GA 30093
USA

tel 1–770–662–3002
fax 1–770–447–1036

e-mail: info@bosphoruscymbal.com
website: www.bosphoruscymbal.com

Chalklin Percussion Mallets

Paul Chalklin started his company in 1971 and produces quality timpani, tuned percussion, bass drum, gong, and tam-tam mallets for players and companies all over the world. In addition, after a long association with Italian opera houses, he rents out the Campanelli Giapponese and the cast-tuned gongs for Puccini's *Madame Butterfly* and *Turandot*.

Chalklin Percussion
Southern Cross, The Ridgeway
Chiseldon, Swindon
Whiltshire SN4 0HT
England

fax 44–(0)1793–741212

Tony Charles

Longtime expert maker of the whole range of steel drums.

Tony Charles
231 Grange Road
London SE25 6TH

tel/fax 44–(0)208–8771–2622

De Gouden Brug BV

Lee H. Kuijpers began tuning Orff instruments in 1962 and eventually established De Gouden Brug (The Golden Bridge) in 1970. The company now manufactures a vast range of Orff Schulwerk percussion, including glockenspiels, xylophones, and metallophones in both diatonic and chromatic form.

De Gouden Brug BV
Postbus 214
120 AE Hilversum
Holland

Early Music Shop

The Early Music Shop was founded in 1968 at the start of the reawakening of interest in early music being made on period instruments or accurate copies. It has now become a source of early music instruments by makers from all over the world, and the catalogue includes keyboards, strings, woodwind, and brass as well as percussion. For the percussionist there are nakers, tabors, timbrels, and medieval and Renaissance drums.

The Early Music Shop
38 Manningham Lane
Bradford
West Yorks BD13 EA
England

tel 44–(0)1274–393753
fax 44–(0)1274–393516

e-mail: sales@earlyms.demon.co.uk
website: www.e-m-s.com

Fall Creek Marimbas

Bill Youhass founded Fall Creek Marimbas in 1972 when he was teaching percussion at Ithaca College School of Music, having just spent two years learning to build marimbas. However, fate decreed that it was glockenspiels rather than marimbas that would become his prime interest. After research into just what made the old Leedy and Deagan glockenspiels so successful, he began to produce the instruments that are now so popular with many of the world's top orchestras. In addition he is renowned for his work on tuning all the keyboard percussion and is sought after all over the world. The glockenspiels are built in conjunction with Brian Stotz of Repaircussions, who make the cases.

Fall Creek Marimbas
1445 Upper Hill Road
Middlesex, NY 14507
USA

tel 1–716–554–4011
fax 1–716–554–4017

e-mail: pangaia@earthlink.net
website: www.marimbas.com

Finkenbeiner Inc.

American source for glass instruments.

G. Finkenbeiner Inc.
33 Rumford Ave.
Waltham, MA 02452
USA

tel 1–781–642–0461
fax 1–781–647–4044

e-mail: gfiglass@erols.com
website: www.finkenbeiner.com/links.html

Vic Firth Inc.

Vic Firth was for many years the world-renowned timpanist of the Boston Symphony Orchestra. But apart from playing, he founded a company that produces a wide range of mallets that are popular with professionals worldwide.

Vic Firth Inc.
65 Commerce Way
Dedham, MA 02026–2953
USA

tel 1–781–326–3455
fax 1–781–326–1273

e-mail: lfo@vicfirth.com
website: www.vic-firth.com

Giannini Swiss Drums

Giannini Swiss Drums, formerly Giannini Trommelbau, is a sixty-year-old company specializing in drumkits, snare drums, bass drums, Basler trommel, and orchestral chimes.

Giannini Swiss Drums
Aegertenstrasse 8
CH–8803 Zurich
Switzerland

tel 41–(0)1–461–7643
fax 41–(0)1–461–7478

website: www.giannini-drums.ch

Gope Instrumentos Musicals

Gope manufacture a wide range of Latin percussion instruments and effects.

Gope Instrumentos Musicals
Rua-Benedito Fernandes, Centro
06900–000 FMBU GUACU-SP_Brazil

tel 55–(0)11–4661–7000
fax 55–(0)–11–4661–1700

e-mail: gope@gope.net
website: www.gope.net

Grover Pro Percussion

Grover Pro Percussion was founded by Neil Grover in 1978, and although it has a relatively small range of products it is another company whose size belies its importance. Grover instruments and mallets are used by many of the world's top orchestras and players; instruments supplied include tambourines, triangles, snare drums, woodblocks, and a wide range of mallets and beaters.

Grover Pro Percussion
22 Prospect Street, Unit 7
Woburn, MA 01801
USA

tel 1–781–935–°6200
fax 1–781–935–5522

e-mail: grover@tiac.net
website: www.groverpro.com

JAS Musicals Ltd.

JAS Musicals specialize in all Indian instruments for the percussionist, including a wide variety of dhols, tabla, dholaks, etc.

JAS Musicals Ltd.
108A The Broadway
Southall
Middlesex UB1 1QF
England

tel. 44–(0)20–8574–2686
fax 44–(0)20–8571–7445

e-mail: harjit@jas-musicals.com
website: www.jas-musicals.com

Kambala Percussion

Kambala Percussion specialize in handmade quality instruments from the African Ivory Coast. The catalogue includes five sizes of djembe solo, eight sizes of traditional djembe, shekere, waterdrum, balafon, kring, doumdoum, bougarabou, berimbau, oprente, and all types of African hand percussion instruments.

Kambala Percussion
Ganslestrasse 3

A–6890 Lustenau
Austria

tel/fax 43–(0)5577–84836

Kolberg Percussion

Kolberg Percussion was founded by Bernhard Kolberg in 1968. As a percussionist and engineer he is uniquely qualified, and the influence of Kolberg Percussion today is very far-reaching. It is in developing and extending existing instruments that this influence is so apparent, and percussionists and composers alike visit the Kolberg showroom near Stuttgart to browse around this veritable Aladdin's den to look for his latest innovations. Apart from all the normal percussion instruments, including virtually every type of drum, stand, and effect, the catalogue includes snare drum with pedal snare release, mounted tambourine, with endless thumb trill facility, and unique choice of jingle type, a range of steel drums, five sizes of triangle in five different metals, chromatic sets of motor horns, woodblocks, temple blocks, log drums, anvils, anklung, lithophone, boobams (three octaves), flaschenspiel/bouteillephone (three octaves), handbells (three octaves), crotales (five octaves), cowbells (four octaves), pedal glockenspiel (three octaves), celeste (five and a half octaves), keyed glockenspiel (three and a half octaves), bell plates (five octaves), tubular bells/chimes (one and a half, two, and three octaves), Thai gongs (four octaves), and Turandot gongs. They also make top-class professional timpani with many refinements, as well as standard professional, soloist, and baroque models.

In addition, Kolberg manufacture all the orchestral hardware, from flight cases to music stands, and chairs and stools of all types. The catalogue is far and away *the* most comprehensive, and Kolberg is well established as one of the most important and influential names in contemporary world percussion.

One of Bernhard Kolberg's latest ideas is to establish a museum for percussion, and he already has an amazing collection of instruments which will fascinate any percussion enthusiast.

Kolberg Percussion GmbH
Stuttgarter Strasse 157
D-73066 Uhingen
Germany

tel 49–(0)7161/30–05–30
fax 49–(0)7161/30–05–40

Kozmosz Ipari

The famous cimbalom maker Istvan Jancso works with this company in Budapest.

Kozmosz Kultürcikk és fémárukat Byártó
Ipari Szövetkezet

1065 Budapest, Haos u. 25
Hungary

tel 36–(0)312–4211
fax 36–(0)312–0831

e-mail: kozmosz@matavnet.hu

Lefima

Lefima is Germany's oldest percussion company, and dates back to 1861 when it was set up by Ernst Leberecht Fischer. Its programme today includes instruments for education and music therapy, and a special historic line called percussion Antiqua. There is a very comprehensive range of marching percussion instruments, including Basler trommel, a range of marching percussion instruments, including Basler trommel, a range of concert snare, tenor, and bass drums, nakers, Baroque timpani, and a complete range of pedal timpani through to top professional models. It also makes a "four-row" xylophone, conventional keyboard style three- and three-and-a-half-octave xylophones, two-and-a-half- and three-octave glockenspiels, with or without pedal, Afro and Latin percussion instruments and effects, flight cases and covers, and a full range of stands and mallets.

Lefima Percussion
Leberecht Fischer KG
Postfach 1251
D-8490
Cham
Germany

tel 49–(0)9971–32081
fax 49–(0)9971–31122

e-mail: aehnelt@mail.teleconsult.de
website: www.lefima.com/history.html

LP Music Group

LP (Latin Percussion) was founded by Martin Cohen in 1964, and today is a major force in world percussion. Innovation has always been a strong point with LP, and the vibraslap (instead of the jawbone) and metal bead afuche or cabaca (instead of the bead lattice on a gourd) are just two instruments that started life with LP and have since been widely copied. The fragility of both the original effects has led to worldwide acceptance of the LP substitutes as instruments in their own right. The traditional afuche is of course also still very prominent, but the vibraslap has virtually taken over completely from the quijada or jawbone. Today, LP markets a wide range of drums and effects: various bongos and congas in both wood and fibreglass, timbales, timbalitos, djembe, talking drums, bata drums, udu drums, all types of cowbells and mark trees, agogos, blocks, tambourines, trian-

gles, sleighbells, shakers, guiros, maracas, drumkits, gongs, and cymbals, plus marching and student percussion.

LP Music Group
160 Belmont Avenue
Garfield, NJ 07026
USA

tel 1–973–478–6903
fax 1–973–772–3568

website: www.lpmusic.com

Ludwig Musser

The Ludwig Drum Company was founded in 1909 by William and Theobald Ludwig in a Chicago garage. The brothers, both accomplished percussionists, manufactured and patented the first bass drum foot pedal in that inaugural year. The company also produced sound effects for silent films. The following years saw a variety of further innovations, from the Super Sensitive snare strainer to the first custom-built drumkit, and on to the famous Black Beauty snare drum. Later, around 1930, came one of their most important inventions in the "balanced-action" mechanism for pedal timpani. Ludwig were also at the forefront of the American marching band tradition, and of percussion in education. In 1966 Ludwig merged with the Musser Marimba Company, who manufactured tuned percussion instruments, and around 1970 they acquired the famous name in German timpani making of Gunter Ringer. The craftsman from Berlin took his expertise to Chicago, and Ringer timpani have been a notable feature of the Ludwig catalogue ever since. Ludwig today manufacture both Ringer and the balanced-action pedal timpani, five-, four-and-two-thirds, four-and-a third-, and four-octave marimbas, three-octave vibraphones, three-and-a-half- and three-octave xylophones, one-and-a half-octave chimes, two-and-a-half-octave glockenspiels, concert snare drums and bass drums, concert toms, drumkits, and a full range of educational and marching band instruments.

Ludwig Musser
PO Box 310
Elkhart, IN 46515–0310
USA

tel 1–219–522–1675
fax 1–219–522–0334

Majestic Percussion

The Dutch family firm of van der Glas BV was founded in 1921 by Willem Klazes van der Glas, the grandfather of the present owner Wim van der Glas. Situated in Heerenveen, the company originally only sold organs, pianos, and wind instruments, but production of percussion instruments soon followed. The Majestic brand name was introduced in the 1960s, and the company now produces a very full range of marching percussion instruments (including xylophone and marimba), and also drumsets, snare drums, and concert toms, a range of concert bass drums, one-and-a-half-octave sets of bells (chimes), school/band basic pedal timpani with fold-away pedal, and top-of-the-range professional timpani in various formats.

van der Glas BV Percussion Instruments
Pastorielaan 4a/PO Box 85
8440 AB Herrenveen
The Netherlands

tel 31–(0)5136–26450
fax 32–(0)5136–22652

e-mail: info@majestic-percussion.com
website: www.majestic-percussion.com

Malletech

Malletech is an American company founded by marimba virtuoso Leigh Howard Stevens in 1991 to produce instruments of the quality now demanded by today's soloists. The company became part of Avedis Zildjian in 1997. The range currently includes five-, four-and-two-thirds-, and four-and-a-third-octave marimbas, a two-octave bass marimba, four- and three-and-a-half-octave xylophones, and two-and-a-half-octave glockenspiels, plus a range of mallets.

Malletech
PO Box 467
Asbury Park, NJ 07732
USA

tel 1–732–774–0088
fax 1–732–774–0033

Marimba One

As might be expected from the name, Marimba One is a specialist company producing marimbas, and was founded in 1982 by Ron Samuels. Though only having a minor association with percussion generally, he was attracted to the idea of building quality marimbas, and today the reputation of Marimba One speaks for itself. The instruments are custom-made, and the range includes four-and-a-third-, four-and-two-thirds-, and five-octave and bass marimbas. Baritone and tenor balaphones are also available, modeled on the Shona balaphones of Zimbabwe.

Marimba One
PO Box 786

Arcarta, CA 95518
USA

tel 1–707–822–9570
fax 1–707–822–6256

e-mail: percussion@marima1.com
website: 222.marimba1.com

Marcus de Mowbray

Marcus de Mowbray has a unique concept with his tour timps. Even fibreglass-shell timpani still have the problem of their sheer physical bulk, but tour timps solve both weight and size problems, having no shell—just the drum head, folding frame, and pedal, in diameters from 32" to 22½". He also makes a lightweight drumkit and various snare drums.

Marcus de Mowbray
330 St James's Road Studios
London SE1 5JX
England

tel/fax 44–(0)20–74032–9733

e-mail: marcusdem@hotmail.com

Meinl Musikinstrumente

Meinl started life in 1979 and has grown to be an important player in the ever-growing percussion scene. Its catalogue now includes a range of cymbals, plus congas, congitas, bongos, and djembes (both in traditional timber and fibreglass), timbales, batas, qweekas, talking drums, and a very full range of effects.

Roland Meinl Musikinstrumente GmBH & Co.
An den Herrenbergen 24
91413 Neustadt a.d. Aisch
Germany

tel 49–(0)9161–7880
fax 49–(0)9161–3906

e-mail: meinl@t-online.de
website: www.meinl.de

Paiste

Today Paiste is one of the key players in cymbal, gong, and tam-tam manufacturers. The company originated in 1909 in St. Petersburg, and, after moves brought about by the volatile political situation in Europe in the first half of the twentieth century, factories were opened in Rendsburg in

Germany in 1951 and in Nottweil, Switzerland, in 1957. Paiste now produce a huge range of all types of cymbal, tam-tams from 20" to 79", various types of gong, a four-octave range of tuned gongs, two octaves of crotales, two octaves of tuned discs, and a range of mallets. Paiste tam-tams are used by a great many professional orchestras; they are decorated with Chinese characters, which roughly translate as "The good shall come. The bad shall go."

Paiste GmbH & Co. KG
Gorch-Fock-Strasse 13
D-2373 Schacht-Audorf
Germany

tel. 49–(0)4331–90–01

Paiste AG
Kantonsstrasse 2
CH–6207 Nottwiel
Switzerland

tel 41–(0)939–3333
fax 41–(0)939–336

Paiste America Inc.
460 Atlas Street
Brea, CA 92621
USA

tel 1–714–529–2222

Pearl

Pearl is a large Japanese company, now well established as a key player on the percussion scene worldwide. Their catalogue includes a wide range of concert snare drums, concert toms, cymbals, Latin percussion, drumsets and marching percussion, plus many stands and accessories. Additionally, in the U.S. they offer the complete range of Adams timpani and tuned percussion.

Pearl Corporation
10–2–1 Yachiyo-Dai Nishi
Yachiyo, Chiba 276
Japan

Pearl Corporation
549 Metroplex Drive
PO Box 11240
Nashville, TN 37211-3140

tel 1–615–833–4477
fax 1–615–833–6242

Pearl (UK) Ltd.
Sherbourne Drive
Tilbrook, Milton

Keynes MK7 8AP
Australia

tel 44–(0)1908-366941
fax 44–(0)1908–640655

website: www.pearldrum.com

Percussion Plus

Percussion Plus started life in 1987 and has established a reputation for quality instruments. They stock a wide and very imaginative range of education and music therapy instruments, plus drumkits, accessories, Latin percussion, and a variety of world percussion, and also some tuned percussion, including one-and-a-half-octave chimes with 1" tubes.

Percussion Plus
Ludlow Hll Road
West Bridgford
Nottingham NG2 6HD
England

tel 44–(0)115–936–0450
fax 44–(0)115–945–2365

website: www.percussionplus.co.uk

Petit & Fritsen

The Dutch royal bell foundry Petit & Fritsen dates back to 1660—another company with a long and fascinating history. Today they produce church bells, carillons, clock chimes, handbells, etc., and have provided cast bells for several symphony orchestras and opera houses.

Petit & Fritsen Ltd.
PO Box 2
5735 ZG Aarle-Rixtel
The Netherlands

tel 31–(0)4923–81287
fax 31–(0)4923–83195

e-mail: petit.fritsen@wxs.nl
website: www.petit.fritsen.nl

PJ Drums and Percussion

PJ Drums and Percussion was founded in 1980 by Peter Kragh-Jacobsen and Ole Randboll and has developed to become a very valued and influential player on the contemporary percussion scene. PJ has a very comprehensive range of Latin percussion, from congas, timbales, and bongos to surdos, repiniques, pandeiros, cuicas, and tarols, plus snare drums and many orchestral effects. They also stock tabla, Sri Lankan drums, djembe, darabuka, and steel drums.

PJ Drums and Percussion
Frederiksberg Bredegardel
DK–2000 Copenhagen F
Denmark

tel 45–37–10–5710
fax 45–38–33–2442

e-mail: piperc@image.dk
website: www.piperc.dk

Potter & Co.

George Potter & Co. is an English company dating back to 1810, manufacturing drums, flutes, and bugles for military bands. The company is based at Aldershot, the home of the British army. Potter actually took out a patent for tensioning drum heads by rods rather than rope in the early 1830s, but the army traditionalists rejected the idea—it didn't look right and it broke with tradition. Amazingly, this opposition and rod-tensioned drums prevailed for another 140 years until the 1950s! Today, Potter is still thriving, making all types of drum for military bands, adding badges and emblazonments, and also silver and silverine shells as required. With their traditional drum-making skills, they also make drums to order, including Baroque timpani, for the orchestral world.

George Potter & Co. Ltd.
26–8 Grosvenor Road
Aldershot
Hants/GU11 3DP
England

tel 44–(0)1252–323226
fax 44–(0)1252–342921

e-mail: pottersdrums@aol.com

Premier Percussion

Premier Percussion was founded in 1922 by Albert della Porta, a dance-band drummer, and his assistant George Smit. Based at Wigston in England, it remains a force in world percussion. Briefly taken over by Yamaha in 1987, it regained independence in 1993. Premier currently market a comprehensive range of drumkits and marching percussion. Orchestrally they offer a range of timpani, three-and-a-half- and four-octave xylophones, four-octave marimbas, three-octave vibraphones, two-and-a-half-octave glockenspiels, one-and-a-half-octave bells/chimes, concert bass, and snare drums.

Premier Percussion
Blaby Road, Wigston
Leicester LE18 4DF
England

tel 44–(0)–116–277–3121
fax 44–(0)–116–227–6627

Premier Percussion USA Inc.
1263 Glen Avenue
Suite 250
Moorestown, NJ 07057
USA

tel 1–609–231–8825
fax 1–609–231–8829

website: www.premier-percussion.com

Professional Percussion

Professional Percussion is a company providing all types of Japanese drums and percussion.

2–37–21 Koenji-minami
Suginami-ku
Tokyo 166–0003
Japan

tel 81–(0)3–3314–6811
fax 81–(0)3–3314–0578

e-mail: pp@pro-perc.co.jp
website: www.pro-per.co.jp

Remo

Remo Belli took up drumming at the age of 10, turned professional at 16, and was soon touring and recording with many of the top musicians of the time. Seeing a gap in the market, he opened his store Drum City in Hollywood in 1952. In the mid-1950s he became aware of a new plastic material called mylar being manufactured by DuPont, and 1957 saw the first appearance of the plastic drum- and timpani heads which were to revolutionize drumming and percussion, and the establishment of Remo Inc. Since that time Remo has never looked back, and today their huge variety of plastic drumheads ensure that they remain a world leader. In 1968 Remo started producing rototoms, and they have now gone on to make Western copies of many ethnic drums such as djembes, surdos, congitas, congas, and talking drums. They also manufacture a comprehensive range of drumkits, accessories, and children's percussion.

Remo Inc.
28101 Industry Drive
Valencia, CA 91355
USA

tel 1–805–294–5600
fax 1–805–294–5700

Sabar Roots Percussion

Sabar Roots is another company specializing mainly in African drums and effects. They stock djembe in several sizes, Senegalese drums, bougarabou, waterdrums, talking drums, balafon, kalimbas, steel drums, and all types of rattles and shekere.

Sabar Roots Percussion
Sielwall 7
D–2800 Bremen 1
Germany

tel 49–(0)421–73475
fax 49–(0)421–71867

Sabian

Sabian is now one of the world's top cymbal manufacturers. The Sabian plant at Meductic, North Brunswick, in Canada started life in 1968 as a Zildjian factory producing Zildjian and Zilco cymbals. The Avedis Zildjian of the famous Turkish cymbal-making family who set up business in the early twentieth century near Boston, Massachusetts, died in 1979, and the company passed to his two sons, Armand and Robert. Eventually the differences between the two brothers became irreconcilable, and after protracted legal negotiations Robert Zildjian set up Sabian (from the names of his three children SAlly, BIlly, and ANdy) in 1982, though the company wasn't allowed into the American market until 1983. Today, Sabian is a key player in the huge cymbal market, and they produce cymbals for every type of music and for many of the big names in drumming and percussion. They also have Chinese gongs, tam-tams (the largest is 28"), finger cymbals, ice bells, two small thundersheets, cymbal discs, and two octaves of crotales.

Sabian Ltd.
219 Main Street
Meductic
New Brunswick E6H 21.5
Canada

tel 1–(0)506–272–2019
fax 1–(0)506–272–2040

website: www.sabian.com

Sascha Reckert

Sascha Reckert is the leader of the glass instrument group Sinfonia di Vetro and builds all the glass instruments with the support of the glass company Eisch in Frauenau, Germany. Enquiries for glass instruments to

Sascha Reckert
Am Strutenanger 3b
D–85764 Oberschleissheim
Germany

tel 49–(0)89–31598720
fax 49–(0)89–3150154

Schiedmayer

One of the principal manufacturers of the celeste.

Schiedmayer Celestabau GmbH Stuttgart
Lenbachstrasse 53
70192 Stuttgart
Germany

tel 49–(0)711–135–33–60
fax 49–(0)711–135–33–613

e-mail: schiedmayer@pianos.de
website: www.pianos.de/schiedmayer/main2.html

Schlagwerk Percussion

Schlagwerk Percussion produces a wide variety of schlitztrommel made from padouk, from four to ten notes per drum, diatonic, or pentatonic, plus "big bom"—similar drums in the bass register. They also have cajons in various forms, a wide selection of udu pot drums, didgeridoos, frame drums, wood drums, woodblocks, kalimbaphone, marimbula, wind chimes, rainmakers, mallets, and a Western copy of the balafon. Another very innovative company extending the boundaries of percussion.

Schlagwerk Percussion Musikinstrumente
Bahnhofstrasse 42
D–73333 Gingen
Germany

tel 49–(0)7162–6066
fax 49–(0)7162–41014

website: www.schlagwerk.de

Sonor

The Sonor company was founded in 1875 by Johannes Link, who from the outset concentrated on producing percussion instruments with the emphasis on high-quality sound and workmanship. After all the political upheavals in the first half of the twentieth century, the founder's son and grandson began again in the 1950s in the small Westphalian town of Bad Berleburg-Aue, with the emphasis on the Orff Schulwerk instruments. Today Sonor offer a comprehensive range of instruments for musical education, plus fibreglass timpani, concert grand marimbas, three-and-a-quarter-octave vibraphones, E3–G6, three-octave glockenspiels, metallophones, drumkits, crotales (one octave), effects, congas, bongos, and mallets. In addition, they now have the Giant Step bass drum pedal—two beaters on the same pedal.

Sonor
Johs, Link Gmbh
Zum Heilbach 5
57319 Bad Berleburg-Aue
Germany

tel 49–(0)2759–790
fax 49–(0)2759–79125

Southern Percussion

The Southern Percussion catalogue includes a very extensive library of percussion music, method books, recordings, and videos.

Southern Percussion
194 Howeth Road
Ensbury Park
Bournemouth
Dorset BH10 5NX
England

tel 44–(0)1202–389793
fax 44–(0)1202–574968

e-mail: sales@southern.perc.demon.co.uk
website: www.southern.perc.demon.co.uk

Steve Weiss Music

Steve Weiss Music is not a manufacturer, but does carry a huge variety of percussion instruments and accessories: the catalogue includes around 170 different snare drums and thirty marimbas for example, plus a huge library of percussion music, method books, recordings, and videos.

Steve Weiss Music Inc.
2324 Wyandotte Road
Willow Grove, PA 19090
USA

tel 1–215–659–0100
fax 1–215–659–1170

Studio 49 Royal Percussion

The officially recognized inception of Studio 49 Royal Percussion was in 1949, though its actual beginnings go back further. Carl Orff, of Orff Schulwerk fame, had formed a close friendship with Klaus Becker-Ehmck who had built a lithophone and a chromatic xylophone shaped like a cradle for Orff's Greek drama *Antigone*. Thus it came about that Klaus Becker-Ehmck formed Studio 49, and the company today is run by the founder's son Bernard Becker-Ehmck. The catalogue includes three- and four-octave vibraphones, all sizes of concert marimba between four and five octaves, three- and two-and-a-half-octave glockenspiels with and without pedal, three-and-a-half- and four-octave xylophones, and a range of effects and mallets, plus of course, a comprehensive range of Orff Schulwerk instruments.

Studio 49 Musikinstrumentumbau
D–82166 Grafelfing bei München
Germany

fax 49–(0)898–54–54–12

UFIP

UFIP was founded in 1931 as the Unione Fabricante Italiana Piatti. Three families—namely the Tronci, Baisei, and Zanchi—originally worked independently in Pistoia, a medieval town near Florence. The Tronci family were originally organ builders, and their craftsmanship was praised in letters from both Verdi and Puccini. Puccini lived in nearby Lucca and would have discussed the making of tuned gongs for *Madame Butterfly* and *Turandot* with them; by this time they were already making keyed glockenspiels and tubular bells. While the Tronci family specialized in tuned percussion, the Zanchis strove to make fine tam-tams and cymbals of a quality to compete with Zildjian. The Baiseis made cymbals of lesser quality for the cheaper end of the market. With increasing competition from the U.S., the three families joined forces in 1931 to form UFIP. They currently manufacture cymbals, tam-tams, two octaves of cast gongs, three octaves of bell plates, two octaves of crotales, bells, and a variety of metal effects, from bell trees to Burma bells to finger cymbals. UFIP continues to have a close association with the Italian opera houses.

UFIP
Via Galliel 20
CP59
51100 Pistoia
Italy

tel 39–(0)573–532066
fax 39–(0)573–532202

Universal Percussion

Universal Percussion is a twenty-year-old company incorporating Cannon, the trade name for a comprehensive range of drumkits, stands, and accessories, plus effects and mallets. They also offer a range of children's percussion.

Universal Percussion Inc.
1431 Heck Road
Columbiana, OH 44408
USA

tel 1–800–282–0110
fax 1–800–979–3786

Vancore Percussion Instruments

The Vancore range includes timpani, four-and-a-third-, four-and-a-half-, and five-octave marimbas, three-and-a-half- and four-octave xylophones, three-octave vibraphones, concert bass drums, snare drums and concert toms, concert accessories, and marching band instruments, including marimbas. The concert keyboard instruments have a unique suspension system using durable gas springs, so that height can be adjusted at the touch of a button.

Wernick Musical Instruments
19 Tichborne Street
Leicester LE2 0NQ
England

tel 44–(0)116–255–6225
fax 44–(0)116–212–8045

e-mail: Wernick@webleicester.co.uk
website: www.webleicester.co.uk/customer/wernick

Whitechapel Bell Foundry

The Whitechapel Bell Foundry can trace its origins back to 1420, and must therefore be one of the oldest, if not *the* oldest, company of interest to percussionists. Originally of course, the bells were cast principally for use in churches. Their eighteenth-century production included a five-and-a-quarter-ton bell for St. Paul's cathedral in London in 1716, a set of bells for St. Petersburg in 1747, and the American Liberty Bell in 1752. The nineteenth century saw a ten-and-a-half-ton bell for York Minster, a bourdon bell of eleven and a half tons for Montreal, and a monster named "Big Ben" of thirteen and a half tons. Today Whitechapel manufactures all types of cast bell for churches, carillons and chimes, and five octaves of handbells, C^3–C^8. (Musical handbells became popular in the late seventeenth century, originally with tower bell ringers. Today, handbell ringing is a popular pastime in many parts of the world, and there are even national handbell rallies.)

Whitechapel Bell Foundry Ltd.
32 and 34 Whitechapel Road
London E1 1DY
England

tel 44–(0)20–7247–2599
fax 44–(0)20–7375–1979

e-mal: bells@whitechapelbellfoundry.co.uk
website: www.whitechapelbellfoundry.co.uk

World Beat Percussion

An American company offering a wide variety of drums and effects.

World Beat
160 Belmont Avenue
Garfield, NJ 07026
USA

tel 1–201–478–6903
fax 1–201–772–3568

Wu Han—Chinalight

Wu Han—Chinalight is a Chinese company with all the traditional Chinese cymbals, gongs, opera gongs, tam-tams, and ching ching in their catalogue.

Wu Han
Chinalight Stationery and Sporting Goods I/E Corp.
No. 910, Ninth Section
Jin Song
Chaoyang District
Beijing 100021
China

tel 86–(0)10–67766688 (ext. 5820, 5821, 5822)
fax 86–(0)10–67747275

Yamaha

Yamaha was founded in Japan in 1887 by Torakusu Yamaha, its initial output being reed organs. Development and diversification over the twentieth century have made Yamaha today a multinational company, marketing not only a huge variety of musical instruments, but also state-of-the-art electronic technology, industrial robots, and motorcycles. For percussionists the range includes top professional timpani, fibreglass timpani with fold-away pedal and legs, four-and-a-third-, four-and-a-half-, and five-octave marimbas, three-and-a-half- and three-octave vibraphones, three-and-a-half-octave xylophones, two-and-a-half-octave glockenspiels, orchestral bass drums, and a large range of drumkits and marching percussion. They also stock five- and five-and-a-half-octave celestes.

Yamaha Corporation
Head Office: 10–1, Nakazawa-cho
Hamamatsu
Shizuoka Pref. 430
Japan

Yamaha Musique France SA
Parc d'Activités de paris-Est
Rue Ambroise Croizat
77183 Croissy-Beaubourg, Paris
France

Yamaha-Kemble Music (UK) Ltd.
Sherbourne Drive
Tilbrook
Milton Keynes MK7 8BL
England

Yamaha Music Mfg. Inc.
Box 1237–100 Yamaha Park
Thomaston, GA 30286
USA

Yuet Wah Music Arts and Crafts

Yuet Wah Music is a valuable source for all the Chinese percussion instruments—drums, temple blocks, cymbals, gongs, etc.

Yuet Wah Music Arts and Crafts Co. Ltd.
143, Wai Yip Street
Kwun Tong
Kowloon
Hong Kong

tel 852–(0)2345–3772
fax 852–(0)2797–0451

e-mail: yuetwah@chevalier.net

Zildjian *see* Avedis Zildjian

Zoltan Szilagyi

Zoltan Szilagyi is a specialist in Jew's harps of many varieties.

Legator-S Kft
Pablo Casals u.9
Kecskemet 6000
Hungary

fax 36–(0)76–475–759

e-mail: jewsharp@mali.matav.hu

THE PERCUSSIVE ARTS SOCIETY

The Percussive Arts Society started life in 1961 in America, Remo Belli of Remo Percussion being one of the main motivators. The aim of the society is to have a positive influence on percussion performance, education, composition, publication, and instrument manufacture. The society has developed from its American beginnings, and today is a worldwide organization with more than 6,000 members; it has its own publicaitons, and there is an annual international convention. Two awards are also presented annually, the society holding a percussion composition contest and electing into its Hall of Fame. The headquarters are in Lawton, Ok-lahoma, with administrative offices and a museum of rare and unusual percussion instruments.

Percussive Arts Society (headquarters)
701 N.W. Ferris Avenue
Lawton, OK 73507–5442
USA

tel 1–580–353–1455
fax 1–580–353–1456
website: www.pas.org

List of Works

Including Players and Instruments Required

It takes little effort to work out the percussion line-up for most pre-1960 repertoire: if the work is Tchaikovsky's Fourth Symphony, there can be little argument with the fact that three players are needed—crash cymbals, bass drum, and triangle. However, the rapid development of percussion in the last fifty years means that with some pieces it may take a lot of time to work out a permutation of players and instruments, and it is now almost obligatory—and very much in his or her own interests—for the principal player to keep a record of requirements. Frequently, different players will come up with varying solutions—this list reflects only one option and is not meant to be definitive. Similarly, the number of drums employed, and which notes are on which drum, is of course completely at the individual player's discretion, and I have therefore only recorded here whether timpani are required. In most professional symphony orchestras the timpanist is separate from the percussion section, and listings of the symphonic repertoire below therefore mention timpani and percussion separately. The instruments and effects listed below demonstrate the huge changes that have come about in the world of percussion.

Abbreviations and Conventions

All specific pitches quoted are written pitch.

bass d.	orchestral bass drum
bass d. ped.	pedal bass drum
cym.	cymbal
d.	drum
glock.	glockenspiel
movt.	movement
perc.	percussion
sus.	suspended
tamb.	tambourine
timp.	timpani
tri.	triangle
vib.	vibraphone
xyl.	xylophone

Abe, Keiko

Michi

solo marimba

Variation on Japanese Childrens' Songs

solo marimba

Adams, John

The Chairman Dances

Written for 3 players; works better with 4.

3 players

1. xyl., glock., tri., bell tree, 2 octaves crotales, tamb., snare d., hi-hat, sus. cym., woodblock
2. glock., 2 octaves crotales, bass d. ped., hi-hat, crash cym., medium and high woodblocks, claves, snare d., sizzle cym., tri.
3. 4-octave vib. + bow, tamb., snare d., sizzle cym., tri., xyl., glock., sandpaper blocks

4 players

1. xyl., bell tree, tamb., snare d., hi-hat, sus. cym., woodblock, tri.
2. bass d. ped., hi-hat, tri., medium and high woodblocks, claves, snare d., sizzle cym.
3. 4-octave vib. + bow, tamb., snare d., sizzle cym., xyl., sandpaper blocks
4. glock., 2 octaves crotales, crash cym., all tri. *except* bars 214, 251, 371

Nixon in China

1 player

bass d., bass d. ped., snare d., tenor d., 2 sus. cym., 1 sizzle cym. crash cym., tamb., whip ratchet, claves, tri., sleighbells, woodblock, 3 temple blocks, rough sandpaper (not sandpaper blocks), ching ching, thigh-slapping (replaces timbales in printed part—composer's change).

Bartók, Béla

Bluebeard's Castle

2 timpani, 2 percussion
2 xyl. (written as "xilophono a tastiera"—keyboard xylophone; the usual remedy today is to use two conventional instruments) bass d., crash cym., sus. cym., snare d., tam-tam, wind machine (not in printed part—stage effect when performed as an opera, but usually required for percussion section in concert performances).

Concerto for Orchestra

timpani, 2 percussion
bass d., crash cym., sus. cym., snare d., tri., tam-tam

Music for Strings, Percussion and Celeste

timpani, 3 percussion
xyl., piccolo snare d., bass d., tam-tam, crash cym.

Sonata for Two Pianos and Percussion

2 pianos, 2 percussion

1. timp., 2 snare d., tri., sus. cym., sharing small crash cym. and tam-tam (with player 2)
2. xyl., 2 snare d., sus. cym., tri., sharing small crash cym. and tam-tam (with player 1)

Benjamin, George

Antara

2 percussion

1. 6 anvils low to high, numbers 2, 4, 6, 8, 10, 12, spring coil, 4 sizzle cym., tenor d., snare d., piccolo snare d., bells (A^4 and F^5)
2. 6 anvils, numbers 1, 3, 5, 7, 9, 11, spring coil, large bass d., tenor d., snare d., piccolo snare d., bells (A^3 and B^3), 4 maracas on foam + 3 others

The composer now prefers rototoms in place of tenor and snare drums, the pitches arranged between the players in similar fashion to the anvils.

At First Light

solo percussion
vib., 2 sus. cym., 2 small Chinese cym., 2 tri., gong (highest A♯), crotales (B^7 and F^8), bow, whip, guiro, large temple

block, small maracas, snare d., tam-tam, newspaper (to tear), ping-pong ball + glass (suitable glass to maximize the number of times ball will bounce)

Bennett, Richard Rodney

Waltz from "Murder on the Orient Express"

timpani, 3 percussion
snare d., sus. cym., crash cym., bells, glock., 3-tone train whistle, steam effect (cylinder of CO^2)

Berg, Alban

Lulu

timpani, 7 percussion + 2 offstage

1. 4-octave vib.
2. snare d., tri., also doubling timp.
3. bass d. + rute
4. sus. cym., crash cym., small tam-tam
5. small and large tam-tams, tamb., doubling timp., xyl. (with player 6)
6. xyl. (with player 5), doubling timp.
7. bass d. + cymbal attached (for clown scene), tri., small tom-tom (jazz drum) 2 starting pistols (6 shots)

offstage: bass d. + pedal, snare d., tri., 5 temple blocks

Lulu Suite

timpani, 4 percussion (1 doubling timpani)
4-octave vib., bass d., snare d., tri., small and large tam-tam, sus. cym., crash cym.

Lulu: Symphonic Pieces

timpani, 4 percussion (1 doubling timpani)
4-octave vib., bass d., sus. cym., crash cym., snare d., tri., small and large tam-tams

Three Pieces for Orchestra

2 timpani, 6 percussion
bass d., snare d., small and large tam-tam, sus. cym., crash cym., tri., tenor d., hammer, 3- (preferably 3?-) octave glock. 4-octave xyl.

Berio, Luciano

Circles

2 players

1. sandpaper blocks, Mexican bean, 3 woodblocks, log d., marimba, 4 bongos, 3 tom-toms, 2 timp., glass and

woodwind chimes, 3 tri., 3 sus. cym. (the lowest being a sizzle), 3 tam-tams, celeste, guiro, 5 cowbells, bells/chimes (B^3, C^4, D, E, F, A♭), lujon, hi-hat, finger cym., talking d. (composer's change—this appears in the score as tabla)

2. 3 tri., 3 sus. cym. (the middle one being a sizzle), hi-hat, crash cym., glass wind chimes, vib., glock., 4 Chinese gongs (F♯^{3}, A, B♭, E♭^{4}), tamb., bongos, snare d., 3 tom-toms, 2 congas, bass d. ped., 5 temple blocks, maracas, xyl., talking d. (again, composer's change from the printed tabla)

Epifanie

6 percussion

1. xyl., vib.
2. marimba
3. glock.
4. 2 spring coils, 2 tam-tams, tom-tom, 5 temple blocks, 3 woodblocks, 2 snare d., bongos, 2 timp., 3 almglocken, bells down to G^3
5. 2 spring coils, tam-tam, 3 tom-toms, 3 woodblocks, 2 snare d., claves, guiro on stand, sleighbells, 5 cowbells, 3 sus. cym., bongos, 3 almglocken
6. 2 spring coils, tam-tam, bass d., whip, 2 snare d., mounted tamb., 3 woodblocks, 2 congas, 3 almglocken, gongs (E♭^{3}, E^3, F^3)

pitch of almglocken unspecified

Folk Songs

2 players
2 sets bells/chimes, 2 × 2 spring coils, finger cym., 2 tam-tams, 2 woodblocks, 2 snare d., tamb.

Laborintus

2 players
2 jazz kits, vib., bells/chimes, 2 mounted guiros, claves, maracas, sleighbells, 2 tam-tams, whip, 2 × 2 woodblocks, 2 × 2 spring coils, bongos

Berlioz, Hector

Grand messe des morts

10 timpani, 8 percussion (this is one solution, not definitive)
bass d., tenor d., 4 tam-tams, multiple sus. cym., crash cym.

Romeo and Juliet

2 timpani, 6 percussion (2 doubling timpani)
bass d., 2 tamb., 2 tri., crotales (B♭^{4} and F^5)
'Queen Mab Scherzo': requires 2 timpani + 2 percussion

"Romeo Alone: Feast of the Capulets": the only section requiring 2 timpani, 6 percussion

Symphonie fantastique

2 timpani, 4 percussion (2 doubling timpani)
2 bass d., crash cym., snare d., bells (G^2 and C^3)

Symphonie funèbre

timpani, 5 percussion minimum
2 snare d., crash cym., bass d., tam-tam, Turkish Crescent (Jingling Johnny); usually multiple snare d. and crash cym., as decided by the conductor

The Trojans

Part 1: timpani, 6 percussion
bass d., crash cym., tri., snare d., tenor d., crotales
Part 2: timpani, 4 percussion (2 doubling timpani)
tam-tam, bass d., crash cym., crotales (E and F), tambourin, tarbouka (darabuka?)

Bernstein, Leonard

Mass

Stage orchestra: 2 percussion
2 drum sets, bongos, crash cym., temple blocks, 2 glock., 2 tamb., finger cym.
Street percussion (i.e., chorus) require claves, bottles, tin cans, tambs., gourds, 3 steel d. (E^3–G♯^{4})
Pit orchestra: 5 percussion, including timpani
vib., glock., 2 xyl., marimba, bells, snare d., tenor d., bass d., 5 bongos, 4 rototoms, sus. cym., crash cym., tris., temple blocks, tamb., tam-tam, woodblocks, anvil, 2 cowbells, timp., sanctus bells, cabaca

Birtwistle, Harrison

Gawain

timpani, 5 percussion + 1 offstage, cimbalom, vibraphone

1. bass d., sus. cym., tri., small gong, large tam-tam, 2 octaves crotales, medium and high woodblocks, castanets, very large Chinese tom-tom (free-standing—Chinese bass d. in part)
2. medium Chinese cym., 2 octaves crotales, 6 temple blocks, 2 anvils, mounted tamb., large sus. cym., crash cym., glock., hi-hat
3. large tam-tam, tri., small Chinese cym., 3 sus. cym., crash cym., 6 temple blocks, hi-hat, bell tree, large guiro (mounted)

offstage: bells (E^3, A♭, B♭)

Mask of Orpheus

7 percussion
total requirement: 2 vib., marimba, 2 xyl., 5 bass d., glock., 5 tam-tams, 11 sus. cym., 2 sets of 7 cowbells + 1 set of 3, 3 congas, 7 metal tubes, tamb., bottom-octave crotales, 2 × 7 temple blocks, 7 toms, 7 high toms, 4 very large toms, 3 guiros, 4 hi-hats, claves, bell tree, 3 bongos, 2 ratchet boards, glass wind chimes, maracas, cabaca, Noh harp, log d. (3 + 7 pitches)

1. marimba, glock., highest tam-tam, 2 sets of 7 cowbells (with congas and marimba) bass d., 3 congas, claves, Noh harp (for player 7)
2. crotales, 2 sus. cym., xyl., tam-tam, tamb., 7 high toms, 7 temple blocks, guiro, bass d., hi-hat
3. vib., tam-tam, 7 temple blocks, 3 cowbells, 3 bongos, bass d., 2 cym. (for players 6 and 7)
4. vib., bell tree, 7 pitches log d., 7 toms + 4 very large toms, hi-hat, guiro, high-pitch claves, ratchet board, tam-tam, bass d.
5. xyl., guiro, bass d., glass wind chimes, 7 sus. cym., lowest tam-tam, whip, 7 metal tubes.

Players 6 and 7 are "floaters".

Bizet, Georges

L'Arlésienne (farandole)

timpani, 3 percussion
bass d., crash cym., tambourin

Boulez, Pierre

Éclat/Multiples

3 percussion; also cimbalom
vib., glock., 2-octave set bells/chimes

Le Marteau sans maître

3 percussion

1. vib.
2. xyl.
3. bongos, piccolo snare d., claves, tri., maracas, small and large tam-tams, medium gong, large sus. cym., 2 sistrum, cloche double (agogo bells or 2 small cowbells)

Notations

timpani, 8 percussion
total requirement: 2 xyl., 2 vib., marimba, 2 glock. (1 to be 3-octave with pedal), 2 octaves bells/chimes, bells (E^5 and F$^{\#5}$), bells (C^4 and F^4), 2 octaves crotales, 4 sus. cym., 4 Chinese cym., 3 sizzle cym., 4 boobams or octobans, 3 snare d., 2 pairs bongos, 2 congas, bass d., timbales, top 6 concert toms, top 4 concert toms, bell plates (B^3 and C^4), 2 octaves cowbells/almglocken (C^4–C^6), 2 small tom-toms, 3 × 2 metal blocks, anvils (1 high, 2 medium, 1 low), 5 small gongs (equal intervals), 2 Japanese temple bells, 5 woodblocks, cymbalettes, small and large temple blocks, 2 medium + 1 large tam-tam, medium gong, log d., bell tree, 2 large tri., medium maracas, claves, glass wind chimes, 2 tabla

1. 4-octave xyl., bells (E^5 and F$^{\#5}$), snare d., sus. cym., sizzle cym., Chinese cym.
2. vib., glock.
3. 2 octaves bells/chimes, glass wind chimes, 2 Japanese woodblocks (mokubio), 2 metal blocks, small and medium boobams/octobans, small and medium anvils, large tri., snare d.
4. 3-octave pedal glock., vib., snare d., claves, cymbalettes, large tri., timbales, 2 woodblocks, 2 metal blocks, bongos, medium and low anvils, bells (C^4 and F^4), Chinese cym.
5. 2 octaves crotales, bell tree, medium maracas, bongos, 2 small tom-toms, high and low temple blocks, medium and low anvils, medium gong (damped), sizzle cym., bell plate (C^4), xyl.
6. marimba (with player 7), top 4 concert tom-toms (with player 8), sizzle cym., 3 sus. cym.
7. bass d., 3 woodblocks, log d., 2 tabla, 2 congas, top 4 concert tom-toms, very low almglocken, medium tam-tam (damped), bell plate (B^3), 5 small gongs (equal intervals), marimba (with player 6)
8. medium and low almglocken, medium gong (damped), medium and low tam-tams, almglocken (C^4–C^6), 3 sus. cym., 2 Chinese cym., 1 sizzle cym., 2 metal blocks, 2 temple blocks, medium and low boobams, top 6 concert toms

Pli selon pli

timpani, 8 percussion
total requirement: 2 vib., 2 octaves bell plates (C^3–C^5), 2 × 5-octave xyl. marimbas *or* 2 marimbas and 2 × 4-octave xyl., 2-octave set bells/chimes, 1?-octave set bells + low B♭, 2 bass d., 3 glock., 7 sus. cym., almglocken/cowbells (F^3–C^5), 6 cowbells (unpitched), 6 gongs, 3 tam-tams, 2 metal blocks, 3 snare d., crotales, 6 bongos, maracas, claves, Chinese cym., 1 rototom

Rituel: In memoriam Bruno Maderna

9 percussion

1. high Japanese temple bell, high maracas, high mukibio, small guiro, tamb., sizzle cym., tabla
2. high mokubio, medium almglocken, snare d., sus. cym., small and large guiro, small and large chocola
3. bongos, claves, chocola, Chinese cym., large tri., sus. cym., sizzle cym.

4. low almglocken, high and low maracas, small and large chocola, snare d., mounted castanets
5. temple block, high-pitch Thai gong, medium and low almglocken, high Japanese temple bell, large tri., snare d.
6. medium tom-tom, large log d., temple block, high mokubio, woodblock, claves mounted castanets
7. small conga, bongos, tabla, tabor, piccolo snare d.
8. and 9. together 7 gongs and 7 tam-tams mounted on 2 racks: gongs suspended *l* to *r* 1, 2, 3, 4, 5, 6, 7; tam-tams mounted 7, 6, 5, 4, 3, 2, 1

Le Visage nuptial

timpani, 9 percussion
total requirement: marimba, 4-octave xyl., vib., 2 glock., 2-octave set bells/chimes, 2 octaves crotales (F^3–$A\flat^5$), almglocken, alto steel drums, pairs of crotales ($C\sharp^4$, $E\flat$, E, A, $B\flat$, D^5, F, B), bass d., snare d., 4 bongos (tuned in semitones), bell plates ($B\flat^3$ and C^4), gongs ($B\flat^3$ and C^4), 2 high and 1 medium gong (pitch unspecified), 1 medium + 3 large tam-tams, 2 congas, log d., 2 tabors, 2 tri., 5 sus. cym., 2 sizzle and 2 Chinese cym., 3 pairs claves, 3 pairs maracas, 2 whips, 4 metal blocks, 7 mokubio, medium and low anvils, 2 guiros, bass bow

1. 4-octave xyl., crotales ($C\sharp^4$), 2 mokubio
2. medium cym., crotales (B^4), marimba
3. vib.
4. claves, maracas, crotales (E^4), sizzle and Chinese cym., almglocken, 3 toms, high medium and low sus. cym., almglocken
5. bass d., medium and low gongs, crotales (D^5), alto steel d., maracas, guiro, whip, 2 mokubio, large tam-tam., tri.
6. glock., crotales (F^5), 4 metal blocks, guiro, claves, sus. cym., gongs ($B\flat^3$ and C^4)
7. whip, tam-tam, 2 octaves crotales, crotales ($E\flat^4$), 2 snare d., 3 mokubio, guiro, claves, medium gong, medium and large tam-tams.
8. snare d., tri., crotales (A^4), 2-octave set bells, congas, 2 tam-tams, 2 medium anvils, 2 high gongs
9. small sus. cym., crotales ($B\flat^4$), 4 bongos, maracas, large sus. cym., sizzle cym., plate bells ($B\flat^3$ and C^4)

Britten, Benjamin

The Burning Fiery Furnace

solo percussion
5 Chinese tom-toms, 3-tone whip, bell lyra in E major + medium bass d. and small crash cym., for other players

Death in Venice

timpani, 5 percussion
total requirement: 2 snare d., 3 sus. cym., crash cym., ching-ching, 2 tenor d., 2 bass d., tri., tamb., 1? octaves bells/chimes + F^3 and $F\sharp^5$, 2 xyl., vib., 2 glock., marimba, 2 octaves crotales, wind machine, bell tree, 3 tom-toms, 4 Chinese toms, rototom (C^4), woodblock, 2 whips, 2 tam-tams, gongs (tuned to $D\sharp^3$ and G^3), assorted brushes/rutes (including scrubbing brush)

1. snare d., sus. cym., vib., bells, glock
2. snare d., tenor d., medium bass d., sus. cym., tri., gong ($D\sharp^3$), xyl., glock.
3. large bass d., tamb., wind machine, bell tree, sus. cym., marimba
4. 3 tom-toms, 3 Chinese toms (+ 1 offstage), ching ching and rototom (with player 5), woodblock, whip, xyl., 2 octaves crotales (with player 5), glock.
5. tenor d., crash cym., ching ching and rototom (with player 4), 2 tam-tams, gong (G^3), whip, 2 octaves crotales (with player 4)

Prince of the Pagodas

timpani, 7 percussion

1. snare d., piccolo timp., anvil
2. 2 tam-tams, tenor d.
3. sus. cym., crash cym., ching ching
4. 2 African tom-toms, 2 Chinese tom-toms, tri.
5. xyl., bells, woodblock, castanets
6. vib., tamb., piccolo timp. bass drum, glock.

War Requiem

main orchestra: timpani, 5 percussion
bells (C^3 and $F\sharp^3$), vib., glock., crotales (C^4 and $F\sharp^4$), snare d., tenor d. bass d., tam-tam, sus. cym., crash cym., woodblock, tamb., whip, tri., castanets, woodblock
chamber orchestra: 1 player
timp., snare d., bass d., tam-tam, sus. cym.

Cage, John

First Construction in Metal

6 percussion, piano

1. glock., highest thundersheet
2. assistant to pianist, needing small and large metal rods
3. 2nd highest thundersheet, sleighbells, 12 graduated button gongs
4. 3rd highest thundersheet, 4 brake d., 8 graduated cowbells, 3 Japanese temple gongs
5. 4th highest thundersheet, 4 Turkish cym., 8 graduated anvils, 4 Chinese cym.
6. lowest thundersheet, 4 graduated gongs on pads, water gong, tam-tam, gong

Third Construction

4 percussion

1. N.W. Indian rattle, 5 graduated tin cans, 3 tom-toms, claves, large Chinese cym., maracas, log d.
2. 3 tom-toms, 5 tin cans, claves, 2 cowbells, lion roar, Indo-Chinese rattle (wooden)
3. 3 tom-toms, tamb., 5 tin cans, claves, quijadas, cricket callers (split bamboo), conch shell
4. 5 tin cans, can + tacks, claves, maracas, 3 tom-toms, ratchet, bass d.

Copland, Aaron

Hear Ye, Hear Ye

timpani (doubling tambour provençal), 3 percussion

1. sus. cym., crash cym., auctioneer's gavel, ratchet, starting pistol, woodblock, castanets
2. tambour provençal, maracas, sandpaper
3. military snare d., xyl., ratchet, tam-tam
4. bass d., ratchet

Music for a Great City

timpani, 6 percussion

1. glock., xyl., bongos, woodblock, sus. cym., crash cym., 2 cowbells
2. vib., glock., crash cym., sandpaper, conga, timbales
3. tenor d., conga, tri., ratchet, sus. cym.
4. snare d., temple block, tri., tenor d., sus. cym., cowbell
5. woodblock, cowbell, timbales, sus. cym., claves, bass d., whip, vib.
6. woodblock, tam-tam, sus. cym., bass d.

Creston, Paul

Marimba Concerto

solo marimba

Crumb, George

Ancient Voices of Children

3 percussion
mandolin part also requires crotales (C$\sharp^4$, G, C^5), and musical saw (frequently given to additional percussionist)
soprano part requires 2 glock. notes, C$\sharp^5$ and E$\flat$

1. large tam-tam, finger cym., crotales (G$\sharp^4$), tamb., timbale? (scored for creole drum), marimba, maracas, small tri., large sus. cym., bells/chimes

2. medium tam-tam, 4 tuneable tom-toms (A^3, B, D$\sharp^4$, F), large sus. cym., tenor d., maracas, bells/chimes (G^3–C^5)
3. small tam-tam, Tibetan prayer stones, claves, vib., timp. (32"), crotales (E^5 and F), mounted top F$\sharp$ glock. note, sleighbells, maracas, large sus. cym., 5 Japanese temple bells

Plus, for other players: glock., mounted crotales (C$\sharp^4$, G, C^5).

Music for a Summer Evening

2 percussion, 2 pianos

1. 3 Japanese temple bells, small and very large tam-tams, maracas, glass wind chimes, alto recorder, small and large sus. cym., cym. with flattened dome to sit on large timp., claves, 3 woodblocks, glock., bass bow, thundersheet, quijada or vibraslap, bass d., crotales (C^4–C^6), African log d., Tibetan prayer stones (much larger than ordinary stones), 2 tom-toms, sizzle cym., sistrum, bell tree, slide whistle, xyl. and bells (with player 2)
2. vib., bamboo wind chimes, 5 temple blocks, sizzle cym., small and large tam-tam, bongos, slide whistle, jug (to be blown), bass bow, bell tree, sleighbells, small and large tri., large sus. cym., xyl. and bells (G^3 and A) (with player 1)

Additionally piano 1 needs guiro and crotales (G$\sharp^4$), piano 2 needs "thumb piano"—American Alto Kalimba suggested.

Songs, Drones, and Refrains of Death

2 percussion

1. glock., xyl., chimes, tenor d., 3 tom-toms, bongos, 3 woodblocks, claves, tamb., 3 pairs antique cym. (finger cym.), sleighbells, small tri., large sus. cym., large tam-tam, small Jew's harp, almglocken (C$\sharp^4$, F, and G), water-tuned crystal glasses (B$\flat^5$, D^6, E, G$\sharp$, A)
2. vib., marimba, lujon, timbales, 2 tenor d., bongos, bass d., tamb, 3 pairs antique cym. (as player 1), 3 gourds, large tam-tam, large sus. cym., sleighbells, Chinese temple gong, 3 tri., flexatone, large Jew's harp, 5 crystal glasses (as player 1)

plus, for other players: 3 tom-toms, claves, tamb., 3 pairs finger cym., 4 sus. cym., large Jew's harp, small Japanese handbell

Star Child

8 percussion

1. small tam-tam + bow, large sus. cym., sleighbells, crotales (A^4, B$\flat$, A^5, B$\flat$)
2. medium tam-tam + bow, very large sus. cym., crotales (B^4, C^5, B, C^6), sleighbells

3. large tam-tam + bow, 3 timp. + metal-edged ruler, cym. on timp., bass d., small and large sus., cym., tamb., crotales (G^5), glock. (with player 4), bells/chimes, claves
4. very large tam-tam + bow, small log d., heavy iron chains, xyl., 4 tom-toms, sizzle cym., glock. (with player 3), vib., flexatone, bongos, wind machine
5. large tam-tam, large sus. cym., maracas, mounted tamb., sizzle cym., sleighbells, 4 tom-toms, thundersheet, 2 octaves crotales, bells/chimes, flexatone, claves
6. maracas, medium tam-tam, sleighbells, sizzle cym., tenor d., 4 tom-toms, medium sus. cym., thundersheet and bells (with player 5), conga, claves
7. large log d., heavy iron chains, sizzle cym., small and medium tam-tams + bow, 4 tom-toms, 4 pot lids or metal plates, bass d., glock., flexatone, conga, claves, tenor d.
8. 3 timp. + metal-edged ruler, cym. for timp., bass d., tamb., large tam-tam, very large bell with metal striker, crotales (C$^{\sharp 5}$), snare d., vib., large sus. cym., flexatone, claves

Debussy, Claude

L'Après-midi d'un faune

2 percussion
Pairs of E^5 and B

La Mer

timpani, 3 percussion
glock., sus. cym., crash cym., tam-tam, tri., bass d.

Delancey, Charles

The Love of L'Histoire

solo percussion
bass d. (dry sound), snare d., medium and low tom-toms, sus. cym., sizzle cym., 3 woodblocks, large cowbell, temple block, mounted tamb.

Donizetti, Gaitano

Lucia di Lammermoor

timpani, 3 percussion + glass armonica
Clash cym., bass d., tri.

Falla, Manuel de

The Three-Cornered Hat

timpani, 5 percussion
2 snare d., bass d., sus. cym., crash cym., tri., castanets, xyl., tam-tam

Fischer, Johann Carl

Concerto for Eight Timpani and Orchestra

solo timpani

Foss, Lucas

Thirteen Ways of Looking at a Blackbird

solo percussion
2 tape-covered tri. beaters, 2 almglocken, superball, flexatone, Jew's harp, 2 smallish Japanese temple bells (to sit on piano strings)

Gerhard, Roberto

Concerto for Eight

solo percussion
4-octave marimba, 3-octave vib., glock., 4 Chinese tom-toms, 3 temple blocks, plectrum, tam-tam, bass d., 3 sus. cym., 1 bowed cym., maracas, claves, whip, antique cym., tamb.

Gershwin, George

An American in Paris

timpani, 4 percussion
Drum set, bass d., sus. cym., crash cym., woodblock, xyl., glock., motor horns (A, B, C, and D)

Giordano, Umberto

Fedora

timpani, 2 percussion
glock., crash cym., snare d., bass d., tri., tam-tam, champagne cork; also tri. offstage in Act III

Globokar, Vinko

Étude pour Folklora 1

3 percussion

1. marimba, 2 woodblocks, gong, tapan, log d., small metal sheet, glass wind chimes, guiro
2. 5 temple blocks, tam-tam., hi-hat, darabuka, sus. cym., tamb., bamboo wind chimes, piccolo timp., sleighbells
3. maracas, baya, vib., tam-tam, 2 woodblocks, 2 sus. cym., claves, tamb., tri.

Étude pour Folklora 2

6 percussion

1. log d., tapan, small tam-tam, zarb (Iranian word for darabuka), 2 woodblocks, medium sus. cym., bongos, guiro, abacus, bass bow
2. marimba, small cym., tom-tom, small tri., gong, 2 woodblocks, metal plate
3. 2 timp., large tam-tam., hi-hat, 6 temple blocks, glass wind chimes, large cym., bass bow
4. medium sus. cym., darabuka, 2 woodblocks, large maracas, tamb., claves, bamboo wind chimes
5. medium tam-tam, small and large sus. cym., sizzle cym., large tamb., large tom-tom, 2 woodblocks, bass bow
6. vib., small tri., sleighbells, claves, small maracas, 2 woodblocks

Gluck, Christoph von

Concerto upon Twenty-six Drinking Glasses

Grainger, Percy

In a Nutshell

timpani, percussion
xyl., marimba, vib., glock., snare d., bass d., cym., tam-tam

The Warriors

timpani, 12 percussion (this is one solution, not definitive)

1. xyl.
2. marimba
3. marimba
4. vib.
5. 4-octave vib.
6. glock.
7. 2 octaves bells/chimes plus G^5 and $A\flat^5$
8 and 9. handbells ($B\flat^3$–C^7)
10. snare d., tamb., woodblock
11. crash cym., sus. cym.
12. bass d., castanets, tam-tam, sus. cym.

Grofé, Ferde

Grand Canyon Suite

timpani, 4 percussion
glock., chimes, vib., sus. cym., crash cym., bass d., snare d., tri., tam-tam, wind machine, lightning machine, horses' hooves

Gruber, H. K.

Rough Music

solo percussion
marimba, vib., 2 sus. cym., 2 Chinese cym., hi-hat, bongos, 5 tom-toms, snare d., large bass d. + bass d. ped., 2 vibraslaps (mounted), whip, 3 small and 3 large cowbells, almglocken ($B\flat^4$–$C\sharp^6$), mouth siren, mounted tamb., 4 timp. (range required: D^3–C^4).

Henze, Hans Werner

Appassionatamente

timpani, 6 percussion

1. vib., military snare d.
2. marimba
3. lead steel d., 3 sus. cym., tam-tam (4 bars before fig. 20; 3 and 6 bars after fig. 22), 2 unpitched gongs (with player 4)
4. tam-tam, 2 octaves crotales, 6 tom-toms, piccolo snare d., thundersheet, 2 unpitched gongs (with player 3)
5. 4 Thai gongs ($F\sharp^3$, G, A, B♭), woodblock, large tom-tom, crash cym.
6. handbell ($E\flat^4$), bass d., bass d. with cym. attached (= sonaglio?), flexatone

Don Chisciotte della Mancia

band: 2 percussion
snare d., bass d., crash cym.
chamber orchestra: solo percussion
mandolin, snare d., military snare d., timp., tenor d., bass d., bongos, tamb., slapstick, castanets, ratchet, maracas, woodblocks, temple blocks, cowbells, sus. cym., tri., bells, small tam-tam, small bells, keyed glock., xyl., vib., wind machine

El Cimarrón

solo percussion
marimba, 4-octave vib., crotales ($C\sharp^4$, F♯, C^5), lead steel d., shell and glass wind chimes, bundle suspended bamboo sticks, 3 cowbells, conga, claves, ratchet, chain to fall on wooden plank and metal sheet, medium and very large thundersheets, bird whistle, 3 bongos, marimbula, small d., bass d. ped., small and large tam-tams, 3 sus. cym., maracas, guiro, 3 Japanese temple bells (high, medium and low),13 rototoms (C^3–C^4), 4 log d. (G^2, A, B, C^3), 8 bamboo d. (Lydian mode, F^2–F^3, i.e. F^2, G, A, B, C^3, D, E, F)

King of Harlem

solo percussion
3 timp., cym. on timp., snare d., bass d., bass d. ped., 3 tri., 3 sus. cym., 3 tam-tams, water gong, lead steel d., 4 temple blocks, 3 tom-toms, bongos, xyl., vib.

The Raft of the Medusa

timpani, 12 percussion

1. vib., guiro in movts. 3, 7, and 8, bells in movts. 3 and 7
2. 3 bongos, bells in Finale
3. marimba, Japanese temple bells, crash cym., in movt. 12
4. 2 tabla, tamb. in movt. 3
5. 5 tom-toms
6. 3 tam-tams, maracas in movt. 14, tamb. and temple bells in Finale
7. 3 almglocken, maracas in movts. 3, 12, 13, and 14, guiro in movts. 6, 7, and 9 and Finale, metal blocks in movt. 15
8. 3 sus. cym.
9. military snare d., 3 tri., woodblock in movt. 9
10. bass d.
11. 3 metal sheets, metal block (not Finale), guiro in movt. 14
12. bamboo and shell wind chimes, metal sheet in movts. 5 and 7

Set players in the order 3, 4, 1–2, 5–8, 12, 10, 11, 7, 9, 6.

Requiem

timpani, 4 percussion

1. 4-octave vib., handbells (C^4, D, F), lion roar, 3 tam-tams, lead steel d., whip, bass d. with cym. attached
2. marimba, handbells (E^4, F, F♯), flexatone, castanet machine, guiro, whip, glock., military snare d.
3. 2 octaves crotales (C^4–C^6), handbells (A^3, B, C♯⁴, D♯), woodblock, tri., flexatone, tamb., 3 tom-toms, bass d., glock., snare d., ratchet, maracas, 2 sus. cym.
4. bells, bass d. + cym., tamb., 3 sus. cym., maracas, snare d., flexatone, temple blocks (C^4–$G♯^5$), whip, crash cym., 3 tam-tams, thundersheet, very high and very low woodblocks

Scenes and Arias from the 'Return of Ulysses'

timpani, 4 percussion

1. 4-octave vib., bass metallophone
2. marimba, lujon
3. glock., tamb., 3 tom-toms, conga

4. gongs (D^4 E, F, G, G♯, A, B♭, C^5, D, F, A), 2 octaves crotales (C^4–C^6), bass d. + cym.

Symphony No. 6

timpani, 4 percussion

1. vib., glock., bongos
2. tam-tam, medium steel slab, bass d., snare d., 3 cowbells
3. marimba, maracas, bamboo wind chimes, chains on steel plate/cym/timp.
4. guiro, large steel slab, 3 sus. cym., tom-toms (C^5, C♯, E♭, F♯, A, B♭)

Symphony No. 7

timpani, 4 percussion

1. bells/chimes, glock., maracas, 6 tom-toms, bongos, 2 small tam-tams; also timp.
2. bass d., snare d., bongos, marimba, glock.
3. 4-octave vib., 2 octaves crotales (C^4–C^6), tamb., guiro, 3 sus. cym., 3 tam-tams
4. gongs (C^4, C♯, E♭, F♯, G, B, E)

Tristan

5 percussion

1. marimba, bird call, finger cym., marimbula, Japanese temple bell
2. 2 alto and lead steel d., castanets, 2 octaves boobams, glock., bird call, 2 woodblocks
3. 4 sus. cym., bird call, 4 cowbells, vib., flexatone, crash cym.
4. bird call, 2 sus. cym., snare d., thundersheet, 4 tam-tams, elephant bells, chimes, bell plates (F♯⁴ and G♯)
5. bass d., lion roar, timp., 2 tom-toms, foghorn

Violin Concerto No. 2

4 percussion

1. 4-octave vib., marimbula, 3 almglocken
2. 3 tom-toms, 4 log d. (E, F, A, B), woodblock, guiro, bamboo wind chimes
3. boobams, bass d. ped., 3 sus. cym.
4. chimes + G^3, 3 tam-tams, maracas, flexatone, Japanese temple bell

Voices

solo percussion
3 timp., timp. + cym., bass d., hi-hat, 2 snare d., 5 sus. cym., 3 woodblocks, chimes (A^3, B♭, B), 5-note log d., 3 thundersheets,

water gong + tub, timbales, bongos, glass and bamboo wind chimes, lead steel d., 2 octaves crotales, tamb., ratchet, marimbula, cuica, 3 tam-tams, vib., Japanese temple bell, cowbell, guiro, 1 octave boobams
Plus, for other players: 3 octaves handbells, starting pistol, wine glasses, Jew's harp, 3 penny whistles, referee's whistle, maracas, claves, chains × 2, woodblock, large temple bell, Eb gong, marimbula, bass metallophone

Hindemith, Paul

Kammermusik No. 1

solo percussion (may be better with 2 if electric siren used)
xyl., glock., snare d., small sus. cym., tamb., tri., siren (electric more effective) sandpaper

Holliger, Hans

Siebengesang

5 percussion

1. glock., bass d.
2. xyl., large and small maracas
3. 2 temple blocks, 4 bongos, 3 tom-toms, snare d.
4. 3 small sus. cym., 3 tam-tams, 2 woodblocks
5. 3 gongs, bell plates (13 pitches required, probably easier to have 2 octaves, C^3–C^5)

Ives, Charles

From the Steeples to the Mountains

4 percussion

1. bells (C^4–C^5)
2. bells (D^2–$D\flat^3$)
3. bells (B^3–B^4)
4. bells (C^3–C^4)

Janáček, Leos

The House of the Dead

timpani, 5 percussion (+ offstage)

1. tri., chains, xyl., glock., snare d., piccolo snare d., military snare d., bass d.
2. crash cym., sus. cym., tam-tam, ratchet, whip
3. sounds of tools, picks, shovels (use anvils half-damped?)
4. sounds of wood saw (use very large guiro or washboard?)
5. bells on stage ($A\flat^2$, $C\flat^3$, $D\flat$, $B\flat$)

offstage: bells ($B\flat^3$–$G\flat^4$)

Kagel, Mauricio

The Compass Rose

solo percussion
   North. Small timp. membrane, bass d., large and very large sheets of metal foil, 2 suspended sistra (one of oysters, one of mussels), very large tamb. (16" approx.), 2 hand drums upside-down with small pebbles, 15+ flint pebbles on soft surface in wooden box, crumpled cellophane in cardboard box, jug + small pebbles, 2 bowls of different materials (e.g. clay and wood) to be filled with pebbles from jug, 2 mounted vibraslaps, anvil, polystyrene around 1" thick—easy to snap, electric fan, large sleighbell, dried buddleia bushes (to wave)
   South. Brummtopf (small friction drum), tamb., 6 bottles (different pitches, laid flat), timbales, pan flute, 2 sus. cym., 3 tri., Jew's harp (as large as possible)
East. Mounted tamb., 2 sus. cym., 3 tri., Indian sleighbells, 2 pairs mounted castanets
   West. 2 African drums (any type), beam xyl. with 6 keys—wooden plates laid across 2 wooden ledges (alternatively balofon), African zanza, vib., early low-built hi-hat + normal hi-hat (Chinese cym. on top and Turkish underneath), 2 pairs African double bells (or 2 agogos), plucked instrument (choice ad lib.), 2 harmonicas with different basic tuning, washboard, wooden log + red-painted axe
   North-East. 4 claves (2 on soft underlay), large cabaca, maracas, chocalho
   South-East. marimba
   North-West. caja India (South American membranophone) or bass d. with 2 or 3 strings attached as snares, kazoo, police whistle
   South-West. 3 different-sized cushions (well stuffed) loose or tied to a table, 2 log d.(4 pitches), conch shell with trombone or tuba mouthpiece, tam-tam, 2 gongs, bull roarer (at least 14" long), 2 different types bamboo wind chimes, anklung, hand-held water jug to drip into large, almost empty, wooden pail (sound to be clearly audible—experiment to produce maximum volume), water drum (gourd in water), lips (puffing) imitating gusts of wind, tape recorder or cassette player (to play pre-recorded tape)
No more than 3 or 4 pieces to be played consecutively in public performance.

Khachaturyan, Aram

Gayaneh

timpani, 5 percussion
snare d., xyl., tubaphone, crash cym., sus. cym., woodblock, 4 tom-toms, bass d. military snare d.

Piano Concerto

timpani, 3 percussion
bass d., sus. cym., crash cym., piccolo snare d., flexatone (written) but it seems musical saw intended

Kodály, Zoltán

Háry János

timpani, 6 percussion
xyl., glock., piccolo snare d., bass d., sus. cym., crash cym., tam-tam, tri., tamb., bells/chimes (+ B♭³)

Ligeti, György

Aventure, Nouvelle aventure

solo percussion
xyl., glock., bass d., snare d., guiro, sus. cym., rack + carpet, table + case, sandpaper taped to floor, sandpaper blocks, resonating box + 4 rubber bands over, cushion, brown paper bags to pop, brown paper, greaseproof paper, tissue paper, newspaper, plastic cup, tin foil, hammer, bottle, tin can, balloons, toy frog, bin/trashcan + crockery to throw in, cloth to tear

Le Grand Macabre

original concert version: 3 percussion

1. 5 timp., tamb., xyl., large tom-tom, sus. cym., large tam-tam, claves castanets, lion roar, referee's whistle, 4 temple blocks, 2 music boxes, swannee whistle, motor horns 5, 6, 11, and 12
2. snare d., conga, 3 bongos, tenor d., wooden strip (to break), woodblock, ratchet, small and large crash cym., medium tam-tam, bells, glock., crotales (E♭⁵ and E), 2 music boxes, metronome, flexatone, bass d., hammer, motor horns 3, 4, 9, 10
3. vib., mounted guiro, whip, woodblock, tenor d., sus. cym., 3 tom-toms, bass d., bells, wind machine, plastic cups, high steamship whistle, military snare d., gong (E♭³), tray of crockery + bin/trashcan, motor horns 1, 2, 7, 8

motor horns numbered 1–12 in ascending order: to be played using hands and feet
complete opera: now usually played by timpani, 6 percussion
total requirement: bongos, congas, ratchet, 2 snare d., high and low woodblocks, 12 motor horns, crotales (C⁵–C⁶), small and large flexatones, wood for breaking, bass d., alarm clock, paper for crumpling and tearing, 2 log d., vib., temple blocks, guiro, chimes, tenor d., large whip, high and low Japanese temple bells, cooking pot, hammer, xyl., paper bag

for popping, medium and large tam-tams, referee's whistle, 6 electric doorbells, lengths of wood, castanets, 4 sus. cym., military snare d., 4 tom-toms, 2 tamb., maracas, claves, 2 hand sirens, cuica, swannee whistle, sandpaper, bow, 5 octave marimba, glock., small and medium crash cym., lion roar, duck call, metronome, bass d. tri., guiro, 3 harmonicas (A, B♭, C), 3 steamboat whistles, wind machine, siren whistle, starting pistol, dustbin/trashcan for throwing crockery
offstage: gong (E♭³), marching d.

Poème symphonique

2 operators
100 metronomes—pyramid type

Macmillan, James

Veni, Veni, Emmanuel

timpani, solo percussion
5-octave marimba, vib., 6 gongs, 2 woodblocks, 6 temple blocks, log d., 2 cowbells, large sus. cym., sizzle cym., bongos, 2 congas, 6 tom-toms, timbales, bass d. ped., large and small tam-tams, mark tree, bells (preferably 2"; E♭⁴, F♯, G, A, B, D⁵)

Mahler, Gustav

Symphony No. 3

2 timpani, 6 percussion + 2 (minimum) offstage
bass d., bass d. + cym., sus. cym., 3 pairs crash cym., snare d., tri., tamb., 2 glock., bells (+ B♭³)
offstage, 1st movt.: 2 or more snare d.

Symphony No. 4

timpani, 4 percussion
bass d., sus. cym., crash cym., tam-tam, tri., glock., sleighbells

Symphony No. 6

timpani, 5 percussion (1 doubling timpani) + 2 offstage
xyl., glock., bass d., sus. cym., crash cym., tri., tam-tam, snare d., hammer, cowbells
on- and offstage: deep bells (written as unpitched)

Markevitch, Igor

L'Envoi d'Icare

2 pianos, 2 percussion

1. timp., tri., tamb., bass d., snare d.
2. piccolo snare d., military snare d., tenor d., bass d., tri., sus. cym., tam-tam

Martinu, Bohuslav

Field Mass / Military Mass

timpani, 8 percussion
military snare d., 2 piccolo snare d., bass d., sus. cym., crash cym., tri., crotales (B^4 and F$\sharp^5$), sanctus bells × 2

Mason, Benedict

!

solo percussion
marimba, vib., glock., lead steel d., caxixi, waterphone + bow, binsasara, cuica, claves, 4 temple blocks, gourd in water, rainmaker, udu pot, maracas, sus. cym., theatre lightning, cuckoo, kalimba, kalimbaphon, large tam-tam, chocola
plus trihorn, 11 small pitched bells, schwirbogen, patum pipes, devil chaser (all provided by composer)

Concerto for the Viola Section

timpani, 6 percussion
1 and 2. glock., vib., tri., tamb., sus. cym., crash cym., bongos, congas, referee's whistle, woodblock, vibraslap, whip, lead and alto 1 steel d., electric siren, 2 mouth sirens, almglocken (C^4–C^5; shared with players 3 and 4), rainmaker, 2 corrugated plastic tubes, 2 slide whistles, 2 small fishing reels.
3 and 4. 2 sets bells/chimes, 2 flexatones, 2 marimbas, cabaca, tamb., ratchet, sus. cym., Chinese cym., snare d., 4 temple blocks, 3 tom-toms, crotales (written C^4–C^6), soft maracas, tam-tam, alto 2 and cello 1 steel d., 2 sirens, C^3 bell plate, almglocken (shared with players 1 and 2), 7 gongs (C$\sharp^3$, G$\sharp$, A, B$\flat$, E$\flat^4$, A, F), 2 corrugated plastic tubes, 2 slide whistles, 1 fishing reel
5 and 6. anvil, flexatone, bass d., soft maracas, tam-tam, xyl., sleighbells, snare d., timbales, low bongo, 2 log d. (3 pitches), bell plates (A^2, C^3), tamb., castanets, vibraslap, sizzle and Chinese cym., cello 2 and 3 steel d., crotales (G^4, C^5, E, F$\sharp$, G), handbells (C^4–C^7), gongs (C$\sharp^4$, A, B$\flat$, A^5), 2 sirens, 2 corrugated plastic tubes, fishing reel, 2 slide whistles

Maxwell Davies, Peter

Blind Man's Buff

solo percussion
snare d., tenor d., bass d. ped., hi-hat, dulcimer, glock., woodblock, temple block, guiro, claves, 2 sus. cym., bell tree, tam-tam, crotales (C^5–C^6)

Eight Songs for a Mad King

solo percussion
snare d., bass d., bass d. ped., 2 sus. cym., tom-tom, hi-hat, woodblock, ratchet, 2 temple blocks, squeak, sleighbells, 3 rototoms, chains, tamb., small anvil, crow call, referee's whistle, wood and glass wind chimes, glock., dulcimer, xyl., tam-tam, didgeridoo, bird whistle, crotales (C^5, E, G)

Revelation and Fall

3 percussion

1. metal and wooden claves, stones, glock., 2 woodblocks, 3 rototoms, 2 sus. cym., bass d., tenor d., snare d., bass d. ped., hi-hat, anvil, referee's whistle
2. glock., metal disc, small woodblock, 2 sus. cym., small claves, ratchet
3. small and large metal claves, tam-tam + soap dish, glass wind chimes, 2 football rattles, 2 whips, bass d., crotales or handbells in D^b major

Stone Litany

timpani, 5 percussion
glock., marimba, flexatone, 2 octaves crotales (C^4–C^6), bell tree, small Chinese cym., small sus. cym. + bow, wineglasses (C^4 and E^{b4}, each on timpani), small tabor, small anvil, very small and very large woodblocks, very small and large temple blocks, maracas, tam-tam, bells (+ G$\flat^5$), rototoms (G^4 and A), bass d., nipple gongs (C^3, E, G$\sharp$)

Worldes Blis

2 timpani, 5 percussion

1. double whip, piccolo snare d., 2 temple blocks, small woodblock, small sus. cym., handbells (D$\flat^4$, E$\flat$, F, G$\flat$, A$\flat$, B$\flat$, C^5)
2. claves, woodblock, sus. cym., military snare d., temple block, 2 anvils, glock., xyl.
3. sus. cym., woodblock, 2 tam-tams, tenor d., claves, bells/chimes
4. woodblock, sus. cym., bass d., piano without action
5. bass d., woodblock, sus. cym.

Messiaen, Olivier

Concert à quatre

10 percussion

1–5. xyl., xyl., marimba, glock., bells/chimes (A^3–F$\sharp^5$)
6. 6 temple blocks
7. 3 tri., reco-reco, whip
8. crotales (C^5–C^6)
9. 3 tam-tams, wind machine
10. bass d.

Couleurs de la Cité Céleste

6 percussion
2 xyl., marimba, bells/chimes, 4 gongs, 3 tam-tams, almglocken (C^4–C^7)

Des canyons aux étoiles

solo 4-octave xylophone, solo glockenspiel + 5 percussion

1. bells/chimes
2. 2 octaves crotales (C^4–C^6) + B^4, $D\sharp^5$, E, and F$\sharp$ bowed, tri., whip, maracas, glass, wood and shell wind chimes, large guiro, geophone
3. 6 temple blocks, claves, maracas, tamb., woodblock, small and large sus. cym.
4. 4 large gongs, conga, large sus. cym., bass d.
5. 2 tam-tams, thundersheet, wind machine

Éclairs sur l'au-delà

14 percussion

1, 2 and 3. each have 1?-octave set bells/chimes
4. 3 tri.
5. wind machine, bass d., tri.
6. woodblock, 6 temple blocks, tri., reco-reco, crotales (C^4–C^6)
7. 3 small gongs, whip
8. 3 sus. cym.
9. 3 large gongs, bass d.
10. medium, large and very large tam-tams
11. xyl.
12. xylorimba
13. marimba
14. glock.

Et exspecto resurrectionem mortuorum

6 percussion
almglocken ($F\sharp^3$–C^7) (3 players), bells/chimes, 6 gongs, 3 tam-tams

La Transfiguration de Notre Seigneur Jésus-Christ

solo marimba, xylophone, and glockenspiel + 6 percussion

1. tri., 3 Turkish cym., crash cym., sleighbells
2. claves, crash cym., maracas, 6 temple blocks, woodblock, reco-reco, crotales (C^5–C^6)
3. bells/chimes
4. 7 gongs
5. 3 tam-tams
6. sus. cym., 3 low tom-toms, bass d.

7 Hai Kai

6 percussion

1. xyl.
2. marimba
3. bells/chimes

4. crotales (C^5–C^6)
5. 2 octaves almglocken (C^5–C^7)
6. 2 sus. cym., tri., 2 gongs, 2 tam-tams

Saint François d'Assise (Tableaux 3, 7, and 8)

10 percussion

1–5. xyl., xylorimba, marimba, vib., glock.
6. bells/chimes, snare d., wind machine, claves
7. tri., 3 sus. cym., 6 temple blocks
8. claves, 3 gongs, tri., tamb., woodblock, whip, reco-reco, glass, shell, woodwind chimes
9. 3 tam-tams, tri., medium and large tom-toms, claves, sus. cym., crotales
10. bass d., geophone, thundersheet, bells, claves

Turangalîla-symphonie

10 percussion
bells/chimes, maracas, tamb., snare d., tenor d., tri., small and medium sus. cym., Chinese cym., woodblock, 3 temple blocks, crash cym., tam-tam, bass d., vib.

Miki, Minory

Marimba Spiritual

solo marimba, 3 percussion
The three percussionists each have drums and metal and wooden instruments of their choice: one plays the lowest-pitched, one the medium-pitched, and one the highest-pitched instruments.

Milhaud, Darius

Concerto for Percussion and Orchestra

solo percussion
4 timp., piccolo and military snare d., tri., sus. cym., cowbell, woodblock, castanets, ratchet, slapstick, whip, tam-tam, bass d., bass d. ped., foot cym., crash cym. tenor d., tamb.

Mozart, Wolfgang Amadeus

Adagio and Rondo K.617

glass armonica

German Dances K.605

sleighbells in C^4, E, F, G, A

The Magic Flute

timpani; also glass armonica

Mussorgsky, Modest

Pictures at an Exhibition arr. Ravel

timpani, 5 percussion
snare d., bass d., sus. cym., crash cym., tri., ratchet, whip, tam-tam, xyl., glock., bell (E♭^{3}; preferably cast bell)

Nielsen, Carl

Symphony No. 4, The Inextinguishable

2 timpani

Penderecki, Krzysztof

Symphony No. 1

2 timpani, 6 percussion

1. vib., marimba, claves, bongos
2. glock., binsasara, congas, claves
3. bells/chimes, whip, 6 tom-toms
4. 5 crotales, 5 woodblocks (written as 'cassa do legno'), ratchet
5. tri., 5 temple blocks (written as 'blocci di legno'), tam-tams, bass d.
6. 4 cowbells, 6 sus. cym., tam-tam, gong, guiro, claves, hyoshigi

Peters, Mitchell

Yellow after the Rain

solo marimba

Philidor Brothers

March for Two Kettledrummers

2 timpani

Poulenc, Francis

The Story of Babar the Little Elephant

timpani, 2 percussion
piccolo and military snare d., bass d., tam-tam, whip, sus. cym., crash cym., tri., tamb., high and low motor horns

Puccini, Giacomo

Madame Butterfly

timpani, 5 percussion + 1 or more offstage
glock., tam-tam, snare d., bass d., sus. cym., crash cym., tri., tuned gongs (D^3, F, G, A, B♭, B, C♯^{4}, E♭, F♯, G♯)
offstage: tam-tam, cannon, bells (A^4, B, D♭^{5}, E♭)

Tosca

timpani, 2 percussion + 3 offstage
glock., sus. cym., crash cym., tam-tam, bass d., tri.
offstage

1. bells (usually played as F^3, B♭, G^4, A♭, A, B♭, C^5, D, E)
2. church bells (E^3, F, A♭, B♭, B), cannon effect (usually 2 bass d.), 2 military snare d.
3. sheep bells, tam-tam

Turandot

timpani, 7 or 8 percussion
gongs (A^3, B♭, C^4, D♭, D, E♭, E, F, F♯, G, A), xyl., marimba, sus. cym., tri., woodblock, snare d., tenor d., crash cym., bells/chimes, tam-tam

Ravel, Maurice

Daphnis et Chloé

Part 1: timpani, 8 or 9 percussion
snare d., bass d., sus. cym., crash cym., tri., tamb., 2 glock., tam-tam, caisse claire, wind machine, pairs of crotales (B^4, C^5, C♯, E, F), castanets, xyl.
Part 2: timpani, 8 percussion
bass d., sus. cym., crash cym., glock., snare d., caisse claire, tri., tamb., castanets

L'Enfant et les sortilèges

timpani, 5 percussion
tabor, tri., woodblock, snare d., bass d., sus. cym., crash cym., ratchet, wind machine, swannee whistle, small and large tam-tams, xyl., guiro, whip, pair crotales (A♯)

L'Heure espagnole

timpani, 6 percussion
glock., xyl., whip, tamb., snare d., bass d., sus. cym., crash cym., tam-tam, sleighbells, 3 metronomes, bedspring (use flexatone?), tri., castanets, bells/chimes (1? octaves + A♯^{3}, F♯^{5}, B♭, C♯^{6})

Saint-Saëns, Camille

Carnival of the Animals

2 players
xyl., glass armonica (written, if unavailable usually on glock.)

Danse macabre

timpani, 4 percussion
xyl., sus. cym., crash cym., bass d., tri.

Samson et Dalila

timpani, 5 percussion
bass d., sus. cym., crash cym., tri., glock., tam-tam, tamb.,
wood and metal castanets
offstage: thundersheet

Satie, Erik

Parade

timpani, 4 percussion
bass d., sus. cym., crash cym., snare d., siren, ship's siren,
tamb., tri., tam-tam, small ratchet, tenor d., 2 pistols, castanets,
xyl., old typewriter (with bell at end of carriage slide), water
splash (pour water), bouteillephone (B♭ major scale in D^5–D^7)

Schoenberg, Arnold

Gurrelieder

2 timpani, 10 percussion
glock., xyl., bass d., sus. cym., crash cym., tam-tam, tri.,
snare d., tenor d., ratchet, heavy chains
*The original version has very poor percussion score parts. A
condensed version of this work also exists.*

Schwantner, Joseph

Concerto for Percussion and Orchestra

solo percussion, timpani + 3 percussion
Solo part, back position: amplified marimba, xyl., 2
octaves crotales (C^4–C^6), orchestral bass d., 2 tom-toms,
timbales, bongos
Front of stage: vib., 1 octave crotales, water gong, orchestral bass d., tenor d., 2 sus. cym., 2 tri., rute, shekere,
cowbells (D^4, F, F♯, G♯, A, B, C^5, E♭)
Orchestral percussion: xyl., vib., marimba, tam-tam,
bells, glock., bass d., 3 tom-toms, 2 sus. cym., claves, 4
woodblocks, 6 tri., 2 brake d., anvil, mark tree, bell tree, various wind chimes

Shankar, Ravi

Sitar Concerto

solo bongos, timpani, 3 percussion
marimba, xyl., glock., bass d., sus. cym., whip, castanets,
claves, conga, tri., Indian bell or finger cym.

Shchedrin, Rhodion

The Chimes: Concerto for Orchestra No. 2

4 percussion

1. bells, preferably cast (B♭^{3}, F^4, A, B, B^5 C^6)
2. tubular bells
3. small sleighbells, tam-tam, pistol (or whip), finger cym.
4. 3 high bells (unspecified pitch), 4 tri. (large difference
   in pitch)

Shostakovich, Dmitri

Symphony No. 2

timpani, 4 percussion
snare d., siren in F♯ (straight note), sus. cym., crash cym.,
bass d., tri., glock.

Smadbeck, Paul

Rhythm Song

solo marimba

Stockhausen, Karlheinz

Inuri

solo rin, 2 percussion
2 octaves bell plates (C^3–C^5), 2 octaves crotales (C^4–C^6)

Momente

includes glissando trommel; other details unobtainable

Zyclus

solo percussion
marimba, mounted guiro, 2 African log d. (4 pitches), piccolo snare d., 4 tom-toms, 2 sus. cym., hi-hat, tri., vib., 4
cowbells, nipple gong, tam-tam

Stout, Gordon

Mexican Dances

solo marimba

Strauss, Johann

Die Fledermaus

timpani, 3 percussion, 1 offstage

1. snare d., glock., bell (E^3), tamb., sleighbells
2. bass d., tri.
3. tri., crash cym.

offstage: A^4 crotales (Acts II and III)

Strauss, Richard

Alpine Symphony

2 timpani, 3 percussion
bass d., sus. cym., crash cym., tri., wind machine, thunder-sheet, snare d., glock., tam-tam, cowbells (unpitched, abstract effect)

Also Sprach Zarathustra

timpani, 3 percussion
glock., tri., bass d., sus. cym., crash cym., bell (E^3)

Don Quixote

timpani, 3 percussion
bass d., sus. cym., crash cym., tri., tamb., wind machine, snare d., glock.

Die Frau ohne Schatten

timpani, 6 percussion (1 doubling timpani); also glass armonica
2 glock., xyl., 5 Chinese gongs (D♭^{2}, D♭^{3}, G♭, B♭, D♭^{4}), bass d., sus. cym., crash cym., snare d., rute, sleighbells, tenor d., tri., tamb., 2 pairs castanets, tam-tam
offstage: wind machine, thundersheet, 4 tam-tams

Til Eulenspiegel

timpani, 4 percussion
bass d., heavy ratchet, sus. cym., crash cym., 2 tenor drums, tri.

Stravinsky, Igor

Firebird

complete ballet: timpani, 5 percussion
glock., xyl., tri., tamb., bass d., sus. cym., crash cym., tam-tam
offstage: bells (E♭^{3} and G)
suite: timpani, 4 percussion
bass d., sus. cym., crash cym., tri., tamb., xyl.

Les Noces

First version (1917): timpani, 2 percussion, cimbalom
bass d., sus. cym., crash cym., tri.
Second version (1919): 2 percussion, 2 cimbaloms

1. 3 differently pitched snare d., bass d., tri., sus. cym.
2. 2 small sus. cym., mounted tamb., 2 tri.

Definitive version: timpani, 6 percussion
xyl., tri., bell (B^4), tamb., tri., sus. cym., bass d. + cym., crash cym., 2 caisse claire, 2 snare d., crotales (C♯^{4} and B)

Petrushka (complete)

timpani, 6 percussion
glock., xyl., bass d. + cym., sus. cym., crash cym., tamb., tri., tam-tam, snare d.

Ragtime

solo percussion
snare d., flat bass d., sus. cym.

Rite of Spring

2 timpani, 4 percussion
bass d., sus. cym., crash cym., tamb., tri., tam-tam, guiro (sometimes washboard), pairs of crotales (A♭^{4} and B♭)

The Soldier's Tale

solo percussion
bass d. (flat, not too large), mounted tamb., tri., sus. cym., piccolo snare d., snare d. and deep snare d.

Takemitsu, Toru

From Me Flows What You Call Time

5 solo percussion

1. glock., vib., lead steel d.(G♯^{3}–C♯^{6}, 2 crotales (B♭^{4} and E^5)
2. 7 Pakistan Noah bells (D♭^{4}, E♭, G, B♭, E♭^{5}, G♭, A♭), 5 Thai gongs (E^4, B♭, C^5, F, G♭), crotales (F^4–C^6), 2 Japanese temple bells placed on 32" pedal timp., darabuka, 6 Chinese winter gongs (A^3, B♭, C^4, D♭, E♭, E), pair crotales (C^5), anklung (C$^{4/5}$)
3. pair crotales (C♯^{5}), 5 almglocken (low to high), 5 roto-toms (low to high), log d. (F♯^{3}, A, B♭, C^4, D, F, F♯, G♯), anklung (F♯$^{4/5}$)
4. pair crotales (C♯^{5}), glock., marimba, 3 tam-tams, 3 sus. cym., anklung (E$^{4/5}$), 3 Chinese cym. very high, medium, and low
5. glock., marimba, pair crotales (A^4), anklung (G♯$^{4/5}$)
6. Japanese temple bells on 2 differently sized timpani (lower, E♭^{4}, B, A♭^{5}; higher, G♭^{4}, F^5, C^6)

Very high-pitched, tiny bells hanging on ribbons of 5 different colours stretched across the auditorium.

Tavener, John

In Alium

2 percussion
high and low tam-tams, high and low gongs, high bells—gliss. over 6 or 7 sanctus bells (composer's change to handbells Bb^4, C^5, E, G, January 1994), bells ($C\#^4$, E, G, A, Bb)

The Whale

8 percussion, including timpani

1. 5 timp., metronomes, sanctus bells
2. snare d., 3 tom-toms, tenor d.
3. 3 bongos, cymbals, bass d.
4. marimba, xyl., hi-hat
5 and 6. glock., sanctus bells, maracas, ratchet, high bell, 3 gongs (at fig. 51)
7. 3 gongs, tam-tam, cym. (p. 22)
8. bells, ratchet, whip

Tchaikovsky, Peter

Swan Lake

timpani, 4 percussion
bass d., crash cym., tri., snare d., glock., tamb., tam-tam, castanets

Symphony No. 4

timpani, 3 percussion
bass d., crash cym., tri.

Tippett, Michael

Byzantium

7 percussion

1, 2, and 3. xyl., vib., glock., bell (G^5), tuned gongs (G^2, E^3, F♯, Eb^4, Bb)
4. snare d., tenor d., medium and large tri., small, medium, and large anvils
5. bass d., bottom rototoms, medium and large anvils
6. crash cym., small and large sus. cym., middle rototoms, claves
7. bells, crotales (C^4–C^6), top rototoms, claves

2 octaves rototoms (C^3–C^5); it is possible to use 3 × 14", 4 × 12", 8 × 10", 4 × 8", 6 × 6"
Some rototom parts for players 5, 6, and 7 together, some for player 6 only; some anvil parts for players 4 and 5 together, some for player 4 only.

The Rose Lake

9 percussion

1. 5-octave marimba (players 5 and 6 also play)
2. 4-octave vib. (with player 5), high sus. cym.
3. 2 octaves bells, xyl.
4. 1? octaves bells (with player 6), glock.
5. 3 octaves rototoms (E^2–F^5) (with player 6), marimba (with player 1), 4-octave vib. (with player 2)
6. 3 octaves rototoms (E^2–F^5) (with player 5), bells (with player 4), 5-octave marimba (with player 1)
7. snare d., small tam-tam
8. bass d., castanets, high and low sus. cym.
9. gong (Ab^2), large tam-tam

Tishchenko, Boris

Symphony No. 3

written with timpani doubling percussion + 1 percussion

1. timp., tom-tom, bass d., tam-tam, sus. cym., musical saw, xyl. (with player 2)
2. xyl. (with player 1), snare d., tamb., woodblock, sus. cym., saw

Vaughan Williams, Ralph

Sinfonia Antarctica

timpani, 4 percussion
vib., xyl., glock., bass d., sus. cym., crash cym., tam-tam, tri., wind machine, bells (B^{b2}, D^3, F)

Varèse, Edgar

Amériques

2 timpani, 13 percussion

1. xyl., bell ($F\#^4$), ratchet (not figs. 33–42)
2. glock., ratchet (figs. 33–42)
3. snare d.
4. tamb.
5. castanets
6. bass d.
7. 2nd bass d., lion roar
8. crash cym.
9. siren
10. tam-tam
11. sleighbells
12. tri.
13. whip, sus. cym.

Arcana

2 timpani, 14 percussion
Part 1: 4 players
bass d., gong, 3 tam-tams, Chinese cym., tri.
Part 2: 2 players
large gong, whip, bass d., tri., tamb.
Part 3: 2 players
snare d., guiro, tri., 2 temple blocks
Part 4: 2 players
tenor d., tamb. sus. cym.
Part 5: 2 players
crash cym., lion roar, large tam-tam, horse's hooves
Part 6: 2 players
xyl., glock., 2 temple blocks, tamb., ratchet, guiro, sus. cym., bell (B^4)

Hyperprism

15 percussion
snare d., Indian d., bass d., tamb., Chinese cym., crash cym., tam-tam, tri., large ratchet, small ratchet, slapstick, large and small Chinese blocks, electric siren, sleighbells + lion roar, anvil

Ionisation

13 percussion

1. Chinese cym., extra large bass d., cowbell, tam-tam
2. gong, small and large tam-tams, cowbell
3. bongos, snare d., medium and large bass d.
4. military snare d., tenor d.
5. high electric siren, lion roar
6. low electric siren, whip, guiro
7. 3 woodblocks, claves, tri.
8. snare d., maracas
9. tarole (small military snare d.), snare d., sus. cym.
10. crash cym., sleighbells, tubular bells
11. guiro, castanets, keyed glock.
12. tamb., high and low anvils, extra large tam-tam
13. whip, tri., sleighbells, piano

Verdi, Giuseppe

Il Trovatore

timpani, 3 percussion + 2 offstage
tri., bass d., crash cym.
offstage: high and low anvils
Requiem
timpani (ideally 2 players for 7 bars), solo percussion
large bass d.

Wagner, Richard

Das Rheingold

timpani, 2 percussion + 12? offstage
crash cym., tam-tam, tri.
offstage: score specifies 3 large, 6 medium, and 9 small anvils in 3 groups.

Walton, William

Façade

solo percussion
woodblock, snare d., splash cym., tamb., tri., castanets, 2 temple blocks

Webern, Anton

Five Pieces for Orchestra Op. 10

4 percussion
glock., xyl., bass d. + cym., sus. cym., crash cym., tri., cassa chiara, almglocken and deep bells (abstract effect, without definite pitch)

Six Pieces for Orchestra Op. 6

bass d., sus. cym., crash cym., rute, glock., tam-tam, cassa chiara, tri., deep bells (abstract effect, without definite pitch)

Weir, Judith

Storm

3 percussion, including timpani

1. cowbells (C^4–C^5), tamb., guiro, glock., vib., bells, medium thundersheet, mark tree
2. xyl., 2 stones, referee's whistle, vibraslap, steel d. (3 unpitched oil d. + 2 alto pans); glock., vib., and medium thundersheet with player 1
3. 3 timp., sus. cym., crash cym., ratchet, small gong, maracas, steel d. (3 unpitched oil d. + 2 alto pans)

Wood, James

Oreion

6 percussion

1. cowbells (C^4–D^6), pair xyl. bars (slapped), 2 medium woodblocks, mokubio or piccolo woodblock, metal claves, medium sus. cym., bowed crotale ($B\flat^4$)

2. xyl., pair xyl. bars (slapped), low sus. cym., bowed crotale (A or A#^{4}), whip
   'D Notation': bongos, piccolo snare d., medium and low tom-toms, mokubio, small bass d. (28"–30"), medium and very large woodblock, 3 simantra, small tamb. suspended in hoop, bottle
3. xyl., pair xyl. bars (slapped), crotale (A^4) + bow
   'D notation': as for player 2
4. xyl., pair xyl. bars (slapped), crotale (G#^{4}) + bow, timp. (32")
   'D notation': as for player 2

Set-up shared by players 5 and 6: 4 Chinese tam-tams (28", 32", 36", 40"), large and very large Chinese cym., additional Chinese cym. or small tam-tam (bar 488), chains.

5. pair xyl. bars (slapped), crotale (G#^{4}) + bow, large bass d., whip, chains
   'D notation': as for player 2, minus piccolo snare d.
6. pair xyl. bars (slapped), 2 woodblocks, mokubio, whip, crotale (G^4 or G#) + bow, gongs—Javanese, Burmese, or Thai—(A^1, C#^{2}, E, F, G, G#, A, B♭; if no low A available use Paiste tam-tam with similar fundamental)

Slapped xyl. bars should be from top octave.

Rogosanti

solo percussion
Javanese gong (A^2): if unavailable use bottom C Paiste gong or large tam-tam struck in centre
A± Japanese temple bell placed on 32" timp.
medium- to low-pitch woodblock or log d., in contrast to simantra
3-octave glock. + 10 extra notes tuned in quarter-tones*
B♭^{2} tubular bell (2" tube), crotales (B^4 and B^5), small bell*, large brass thundersheet, large maraca, 3 octaves rototoms (E^2–F^5) (with player 6), small tamb. (mounted) with sleigh-bells, bamboo clapper (at least 4 pieces, mounted, sprung open on solid base, simantra (or high-pitched log d.), 2 pairs bongos, 4 congas, very large double-headed tom-tom, bass d., bass d. ped., glock. (notes and high bell tuned in quarter-tones*)
* available from Arthur Soothill

Two Men Meet, Each Presuming the Other to Be from a Distant Planet

Solo percussion + percussionist in group
solo part 4 microxyls, cowbells (C^4–E^6, with additional notes in quarter-tones*), 10 wood d. (approx. diameters and pitches: E^2, G, A, D^3, G, B♭, E^4, G, C#^{5}, D#), miniature wood d. (G^5, B, D^6)

Diameters for the 13 drums range from 6" to 31?"
*available from Arthur Soothill
group percussionist vib., low tom-tom, 4 sets bamboos, ekpiri (kernel rattles, not too high-pitched)

Village Burial with Fire

4 percussion only
grand piano, cowbells (B^3, D♭^{4}, F, G, B♭, C^5, E, G♭), 4 crotales (F^4, G, B♭, C^5), 6 bottles (E^4, A♭, B♭, E♭^{5}, G, A), small opera gong, large thundersheet (thin brass), metal shaker, Chinese tiger gong, large timp., ankle bells or ekpiri, 3 strings of bow hair threaded though 3 string groups—E^5, F and G♭, C#^{5}, D and E♭, G^3, G#, and A.
marimba, 4-octave xyl., 4 microxyls, large suspended maraca, sus. cym., bell tree, low d. (Chinese, Korean, or bass d. with calf head), crotale (C#^{5}), tamborim, bow, ankle bells (kernel rattles or ekpiri)
marimba, vib., 4 temple bells (A^4, B♭, D#^{5}, E), sus. cym. (dark sound), 4 woodblocks, ching ching, sistrum, sleigh-bells (high-pitched), large sus. maraca, large tam-tam (preferably Chinese), tubular bell (F#^{3}), ankle bells (kernel rattles or ekpiri)
6" rototom (A^4 or B♭), bongos, 2 congas, very deep African drum, shekere on cushion, mounted 6" tamb., medium and very large woodblocks, simantra, 5 temple blocks, sleigh-bells (high-pitched), large suspended maraca, 4 sets bamboo wind chimes (high to low), bamboo clapper on wooden base, bamboo guiro, high-pitched thin brass thundersheet, ankle bells (or ekpiri), miniature Chinese temple block (C#^{7}), 4-octave xyl., Thai gong (F^2)
crotales (F#^{5} and B), elliptical microxyl
Composer's notes and help with microxyls essential.

Xenakis, Iannis

Persephassa

6 percussion only
total requirement: 4 timp., 5 snare d., 5 bongos, 2 congas, 11 tom-toms, 2 bass d., 2 bass d. ped., 6 woodblocks, 6 metal and 6 wood simantras, 6 maracas, 6 sirens, affolants (6 suspended sheets of heavy tin foil), 6 *galets de mer* (stones), 6 tam-tams (60, 94, 60, 68, 80, and 72 cm), 6 cym. (58, 26, 65, 46, 30, and 52 cm), 7 Thai gongs (E^2, F, F#, G, B♭, C^3, E♭)

1. timp., 4 snare d., bass d., stones, siren, woodblock, wooden and metal simantra maracas, sus. cym. (58 cm), tam-tam (60 cm), affolants, gong (F^2)
2. bongos, 3 tom-toms, bass d. ped., woodblock, wooden and metal simantras, maracas, sus. cym. (26 cm), tam-tam (94 cm), affolants, gong (F#^{2}), stones, siren

3. bongos, 3 tom-toms, timp., woodblock, wooden and metal simantras, sus. cym (65 cm), tam-tam (60 cm), affolants, gong (E^2), maracas

4. bongos, small tom-tom, conga, timp., large bass d., woodblock, wooden and metal simantras, maracas, sus. cym. (46 cm), tam-tam (68 cm), affolants, gong (G^2), stones, siren

5. bongos, 3 tom-toms, bass d. ped., woodblock, wooden and metal simantras, maracas, sus. cym. (30 cm), tam-tam (80 cm), gongs ($B\flat^2$ and C^3), affolants, stones, siren.

6. bongos, 3 octaves rototoms (E^2–F^5) (with player 6), piccolo snare d., large tom-tom, timp., woodblock, wooden and metal simantras, maracas, sus. cym. (72 cm), tam-tam (52 cm), gong ($E\flat^3$), affolants, stones, siren

Pleiades

6 percussion only

1. vib., 2 bongos, conga, 3 tom-toms, 1 timp. (D–C^3), bass d., sixxen

2. marimba, bongos, conga, 3 tom-toms, 1 timp. (A^2–F^3), sixxen

3. vib., bongos, conga, 3 tom-toms, 1 timp. (G^2–E^3), sixxen

4. xyl., bongos, conga, 3 tom-toms, timp. (D^2–C^3), sixxen

5. vib., bongos, conga, 3 tom-toms, timp. (A^2–D^3), sixxen

6. xyl., marimba, bongos, conga, 3 tom-toms, timp. (G^2–E^3), bass d., sixxen

Psappha

solo percussion
high, medium, and low sounds from drums (bongos down to large bass d. and timp.); wood, including temple blocks and simantras; metal, including tam-tams, gongs, plates, etc.